Chester Holcombe

The real Chinaman

Chester Holcombe

The real Chinaman

ISBN/EAN: 9783743334618

Manufactured in Europe, USA, Canada, Australia, Japa

Cover: Foto ©ninafisch / pixelio.de

Manufactured and distributed by brebook publishing software (www.brebook.com)

Chester Holcombe

The real Chinaman

THE
REAL CHINAMAN

BY

CHESTER HOLCOMBE

For many years Interpreter, Secretary of Legation, and Acting Minister of the United States at Peking

WITH SEVENTY-SEVEN ILLUSTRATIONS

NEW YORK
DODD, MEAD & COMPANY
1895

 THIS volume is bound in a shade of color known in China as "Imperial Yellow." It is set apart for the exclusive use of the Emperor, and severe penalties attach to its use for any purpose by a Chinese subject.

The decoration in the upper left hand corner of the cover represents the five-clawed dragon rising from the sea, surrounded by clouds, and grasping the sun. It is thus the symbol of universal dominion, and forms the crest of the Emperor. The figure used is an exact reproduction, reduced in size, of that worn upon the breast and back of all Chinese officials of high civil rank in uniform or court dress. In the design and at the top is an archaic form of the character which means "happiness."

Underneath the decoration is the Chinese title of the book. It was kindly written for the author by His Excellency, the Chinese Minister at Washington, who, however, is responsible for no part of the contents of the volume. It is written in a peculiar style of penmanship exclusively used for book titles.

Upon the back of the volume is the author's name, reproduced from a visiting card, in the ordinary style of writing.

PREFACE.

THE average of mankind resembles too closely that pleasant old lady who lived alone, miles from a neighbor, in one of the more remote nooks of the Green Mountains. A stranger stopped at her gate one summer day for a glass of water. Upon being told, in answer to her question, that he lived in Boston, she exclaimed : " Dear me ! How lonesome you must be away off there !" Boston was a lonely spot in her conception ; but the very centre of the universe was framed within the weather-beaten walls of her cottage.

Like her, we are inclined to measure all people by a yardstick of our own construction, the model for which is found in ourselves. Others are right or wrong, wise or unwise, according as they copy or depart from the fashion which we have arbitrarily set up, the ideal formed within the essentially narrow limits of our personal surroundings.

We smile at and perhaps ridicule the unthinking, automatic regularity with which millions of Chinese drop their winter garb for that of summer, or the reverse, upon a day fixed by the will of one man. Yet how does this act differ in wisdom from that other procedure under which millions of the most cultivated and refined ladies of America and

Europe copy blindly monstrosities in dress or costume at the freaky dictation of an impersonality called Fashion? And if there is a difference in the two rules of conduct, upon which side does the greater wisdom lie? Look at the grotesque outlines and shapes of deformity which have supplanted the graceful contour of the natural woman, and then decide which is wiser, or, if you please, less unwise, for a nation to accept the dictum of one man upon the time when the climate requires a change of garb, or for half the population of two continents, in defiance of their individual taste and good sense, to adopt a whim in dress which may have originated in the slums of Paris or London?

There is need of more genuine knowledge and less narrow-minded judgment. It would, doubtless, be well if we could see ourselves as others see us. But it would be much better if we could see both others and ourselves from a higher and hence more accurate plane of sight, if we could measure men not by ourselves, but by an ideal, a standard man. A greater breadth of vision would serve a more valuable purpose than to increase the accuracy and intelligence of our conceptions. It would make charity more common, patience easier, and belief in the essential unity and nobility of humankind the rule rather than, what it now is, the exception.

It is far easier to criticise the Chinese than to understand them. The points of contact are too few and too recent. Our information is based largely upon fancy instead of fact, and misinterpretation of them and their ways is the easy and inevitable result. Yet they are emphatically a race worthy of serious study. As real life is far more fascinating than any work of fiction, so is the genuine Son of Han, with his fixed and crystallized peculiarities, immensely more interesting to the honest student than the caricatured Chinaman, with whom alone the average public is familiar.

This volume is neither a defence, apology, criticism, nor panegyric. It is rather an explanation. It attempts to give a few of the results of many years of residence among the Chinese, in the course of which the author was brought into close and familiar relations with all classes of the people in nearly every section of the empire. In it an effort is made to describe and explain some of the more prominent factors in the national life, and to show why some of their ways, so odd to us, are natural to them. Facts are dealt with rather than opinions. The book represents an effort to outline with a few broad sweeps of the pen the Chinaman as he is.

The numerous incidents scattered through the volume are inserted with a view to make the picture more lifelike, interesting, and intelligible. Each one represents an actual occurrence, free of coloring or exaggeration. Were it necessary, the place and date of each, with the names of the persons concerned in it, could be given. In the same way, the illustrations are sun pictures, owing nothing to art save the skill and fidelity with which they have been transferred, unchanged even in minute details, to these pages.

Intertwisted with the faults and foibles of the Chinese are many sterling virtues and admirable traits of character. They combine the fixedness of age with the persistence of youth. They change slowly. Yet it seems impossible that any one should come to know them well without reaching the conviction that there is a great future before the nation, and that China has yet an important part to play in the history of the world.

Chester Holcombe.

New York, January 1, 1895.

LIST OF ILLUSTRATIONS.

	PAGE
A High Chinese Official in Evening Dress	Frontispiece
Imperial Dragon	v
Buddhist Devil	v
Pagoda at Pa Li Chuang	vii
Ornamental Street Archway in Peking	x
Stone Gateway	xi
Dragons Supporting the Globe	xiii
Ornamental Fan Design	xx
Dragon Design	1
A Gate of Peking	13
Mounted Chinese Official	20
Li Hung Chang	25
Bronze Open Work	28
Chinese Flag	29
Entrance to the Palace	32
View of Peking	37
Chinese River Scene	44
Post Marking Land Boundary	49
A Lock on the Grand Canal	51
Souvenir Fan	58
Toad Catching Flies (from Chinese Painting)	66
Bridge in Summer Palace	72

LIST OF ILLUSTRATIONS.

	PAGE
Buddhist Female Idol	73
Group of Children	75
Street Scene in Peking	81
Wall About Peking	89
Entrance Hall to Imperial Tombs	92
Jinricksha	93
Carriage of Chinese Official	95
Front of Official Residence	101
Chinese Dragon (Moulded in Porcelain)	111
Sedan Chair	115
Incense Urn	116
Oven for Burning Paper, Confucian Temple, Peking	122
Buddhist Priest Trampling Satan Under Foot	133
Goddess of Mercy	137
Chinese Wedding Chair	143
Chinese Head of Pillar	144
Tomb of the Emperor Yung Lo, Died A.D. 1425	147
Pagoda at Yü Chuan Shan	155
Chinese Catafalque	163
Dragons	170
Head of Buddhist Devotee	171
Peddling Fruit	172
Group of Children	175
Chinese Barber	179
Bit of Great Wall	191
Flag Standards	192
Entrance to Imperial Cemetery	194
Approach to Ming Tombs	195
Bridge on the Grand Canal	199
Street Barrier	213
Ornament Pillar	214
The Great Wall	217
Chinese Beggar	226
Mongol Winter Encampment	231
Top of Pagoda	237
Village on Grand Canal near Peking	241
A Chinese Student	252
Chinese Pony and Groom	257

LIST OF ILLUSTRATIONS. xiii

	PAGE
Gateway	260
Bronze Lion	261
Chinese Passenger Boat	265
The Donkey	275
Chinese Mule Litter	281
Dragons Reaching for the Sun	285
Archway	286
Chinese Jinricksha	289
Chinese Servants	303
Junk	309
Dragon	310
Group of Chinese Workmen	317
Mender of Tubs	321
Chinese Passenger Cart	325
Dragon	330
Antique Chinese Cash	337
Peking-Bank Notes	345
"No Thoroughfare"	350

ANALYSIS OF CONTENTS.

CHAPTER I.

INTRODUCTORY...................................... 1–28

Recent acquaintance of China with Western nations, 1. Date of first treaty, 2. Contrast between the Oriental and Occidental world, 2. Chinese seclusion, 3. Ignorance regarding foreigners, 4. The Chinese Empire and surrounding kingdoms, 5. Position of Japan, 6. The so-called suzerainty of China, 8. Exact nature of relationship, 9. The opium war, 10. Mutual misunderstanding inevitable, 14. Contrast between China and Japan, 17. Discrimination against China and its results, 18. Students at Annapolis and West Point, 19. Prince Kung, 22. Li Hung Chang, 24. No real opposition to the reigning family among Chinese, 28.

CHAPTER II.

THE GOVERNMENT OF CHINA.... 29–48

Peculiarities of the governmental system, 31. Its antiquity, 31. Satisfies the people, 32. It is pure paternalism, 33. Filial obedience and parental responsibility enforced by law, 34. The family the unit of government, 36. The Emperor, 36. Laws are comparatively mild and humane, 40. Rewards and penalties, 41. Two theories regarding the system, 42. Filial piety, 43. Influence of Confucius, 45. Officials chosen from among the people, 45. Similarity between Chinese form of choosing officers and that followed in the United States, 47.

CHAPTER III.

THE LANGUAGE.................................. 49-72

Its antiquity, 49. Immense but uncertain number of characters, 50. Mode of writing and printing, 51. Characters were originally outlines of objects which they represented, 54. Modes of combination illustrated, 55. Idiomatic constructions, 56. Grammar of Chinese, 57. Chinese efforts to learn English, 58. Words lacking in the language, 60. Difficulties of pronunciation, 62. Sounds cannot be represented by any alphabet, 63. Aspirated and unaspirated consonants, 64. Tone has equal part with sound in determining the meaning, 65. Four tones recognized in standard Chinese, 67. Amusing blunders, 69. Local dialects, 70. Pidgin English, 71.

CHAPTER IV.

CHINESE HOME LIFE........................ 73-92

Does not begin with marriage, 73. Lot of young married women, 74. Motherhood a badge of honor, 75. Polygamy allowed, but monogamy the rule, 77. Influence of women, 78. Ties of locality, 80. Chinese not natural colonists, 83. Ancestral worship, 86. Filial obedience, 89. Coffins presented to parents, 90.

CHAPTER V.

CHINESE SOCIAL LIFE.......................... 93-115

Little time given to recreation, 93. An overworked Chinese statesman, 93. Peculiar model of Oriental society, 97. Husband and wife may not ride in the same vehicle, 99. Chinese students in America, 100. Social amusements of Chinese ladies, 102. Women of the poorer classes, 103. Oriental ideas of dignity, 104. Etiquette interferes with social life, 105. Chinese fond of argument, 107. Legend of the fox, 108. Chinese reception-rooms, 109. Dinner-giving between Occidentals and Orientals, 110. The servant of the Corean minister, 113.

CHAPTER VI.

CHINESE RELIGIONS.. 116–143

Confucius not the founder of a religion, 116. He was a sage, not a devotee, 117. Materialism is the basis of Confucianism, 118. Temple of Heaven, 119. Respect for education and literature, 121. Worship of ancestors, 123. What is the practical idea involved, 123. Chinese belief in a future state, 124. Ancestral tablet, 125. All Chinese are Confucianists, 126. Taoism, 126. Its theory and practice, 127. Buddhism, 128. Method of worship, 130. Thibetan archbishop, 131. Living Buddhas, 131. Ideas borrowed from Christianity, 132. Mendicant priests, 135. A pilgrimage to Wu Tai Shan, 139. Chinese Government tolerant, 142. Mohammedans and Jews in China, 143.

CHAPTER VII.

CHINESE SUPERSTITIONS... 144–170

Saturated with superstitious notions, 144. They are separate from religious belief, 145. *Fêng Shui*, 145. Interfered with burial of an emperor, 149. Chinese astrologers, 152. Methods of placating local spirits, 154. The use of pagodas, 156. Lucky and unlucky days, 157. Prayer at the hole of a fox, 158. Prayers for rain, 159. Ling Shih Hsien, 160. Old trees, 161. Inhumanity as a fruit of superstition, 165. Infanticide, 166. Treatment of young children when ill, 167. Two cases, 168.

CHAPTER VIII.

CHINESE QUEUES.. 171–191

Peculiarities of Oriental hair, 171. Admiration of the Occidental beard, 172. Symbol of Chinese manhood, 174. How the queue was introduced into China, 174. It is a badge of respectability, 178. Etiquette of the queue, 178. "Tail-cutting," 181. Chinese belief in magic, 182. Official proclamations giving preventives for "tail-cutting," 183. One genuine case, 184.

CHAPTER IX.

CHINESE COURTS OF LAW.......................... 192-213

Primitive hall of justice, 192. Antiquity of the judicial system, 193. The Censorate, 193. The Chinese Code, 195. Cases are decided by precedents, 197. Dangerous latitude allowed to magistrates, 198. Efforts to secure confession, 201. Antiquated processes, 202. Scene in a Chinese court, 203. Chinese prisons, 205. Modes of punishment, 206. Forms of death penalty, 207. The white silken cord, 208. Etiquette of a Chinese court, 209. A fearful case of cruelty, 210.

CHAPTER X.

OFFICIALS AND PEOPLE........................... 214-236

The Chinaman a philosopher, 214. Official salaries, 216. Illegal and extra-legal fines, 219. Guards against injustice and extortion, 223. Civil-service regulations, 224. Sale of titles and official honors, 225. Power of public opinion, 227. The literati, 227. Dangerous exercise of their power, 229. The Tientsin massacre, 230. Mandarin boots, 233. Interesting case of resistance to oppression, 234.

CHAPTER XI.

EDUCATION AND LITERATURE...................... 237-260

Object of study, 237. Chinese ambition, 237. High moral tone of educational works, 238. Narrow limits of system, 243. Description of course of study, 244. Schools and their arrangements, 246. Method of study, 247. High intellectual ability of the Chinese, 248. The Chinese students in America, 248. Illiteracy in China, 249. System of government examinations originated 1900 years ago, 250. Proscribed classes, 250. Degrees conferred, 253. Regulations for the examinations, 254.

CHAPTER XII.

ETIQUETTE AND CEREMONY.................. 261–285

Politeness universal, 261. Etiquette complicated and tedious, 262. Pompous and bombastic titles, 263. Foreign relations vexed by questions of etiquette, 264. The audience question, 267. The etiquette of a cup of tea, 269. Importance of familiarity with Oriental forms, 270. A Mexican saddle and sombrero in China, 271. Tedious formalities evaded, 273. Lies of courtesy, 274. Chinese habit of repression, 277. Quaint custom among Pekingese, 279.

CHAPTER XIII.

MERCHANTS AND TRICKS OF TRADE.............. 286–309

Grades of Chinese society, 286. Standing of Chinese merchants, 287. Merchants study their customers, 291. Various prices for various customers, 294. The dicker, 295. No standard of weight or measure, 298. Exact book-keeping impossible, 300. Co-operative system, 301. The Chinese "squeeze," 301. Chinese servants, 305.

CHAPTER XIV.

THE POOR IN CHINA........................ 310–329

Intense poverty of the Chinese masses, 310. Average prices paid for labor, 311. Food of common people, 312. Experiences at Chinese inns, 313. Clothing, 316. The house, 319. The labor problem in China, 320. Economy of the Chinese, 322. Government allows begging, 323. The queen of the beggars of Peking, 327. Incidents, 328.

CHAPTER XV.

CHINESE FINANCIAL SYSTEM................... 330-350

The Chinese money unit, 330. Spanish and Mexican dollars, 331. Varying and various ounce weights, 332. Form of silver bullion used, 334. Tests of fineness, 334. Chinese cash, 336. Attempts to tamper with the currency, 339. Doubling cash, 341. Chinese banks, 343. Taxation, 346. Uncertainty regarding total revenue, 347. Taxes payable in kind, 347. Modes of remittance, 348. Needs of reform, 349.

THE REAL CHINAMAN.

CHAPTER I.

INTRODUCTORY.

The commencement of any mutual acquaintance between China and the Western world dates back only a little more than thirty years. The first treaties by which China acknowledged the existence of the nations of America and Europe were signed about fifty years ago. Those treaties, however, only served as a preliminary introduction, and lacked such provisions as would enable either of the parties consenting to them to prosecute any friendly intimacy with the other. So long as not more than three or four points upon the Chinese seaboard were thrown open to foreign residence and commerce, while travel in the interior of the empire was prohibited, Peking remained inaccessible to all diplomatic representatives, and our legations were kept on board men-of-war cruising up and down the Chinese coast—so long as such a condition of affairs existed, we of the Western world could learn little about the Chinese, and they could gain no knowledge of us.

Such was the situation from the date on which the first treaty between China and any foreign power was signed—the British treaty, signed at Nanking, August 29th, 1842—up to the time when, by the treaties of Tientsin, signed in 1861, diplomatic representatives were accorded the right of residence at the capital, and foreigners of all classes were permitted to travel freely throughout the empire.

Then first in the history of humankind two great antipodal worlds of men stood face to face and gazed into each other's eyes. The progressive and aggressive Occidental, quick, eager, and alert, met in the Oriental the very incarnation of conservatism, the embodiment of dignity and repose. Action met inertia. The age of steam, steel, and electricity stood over against the age of Confucius. Let the reader imagine a modern pushing man of business introduced to the Chinese sage, and the two left to become acquainted, and each to gather his impressions of the other, then add to the picture the essential fact that the sage had a positive unwillingness to meet the business man, and he will have a sufficiently accurate idea of the situation.

There was absolutely no common point of meeting, no standing-ground of a mutual advantage mutually recognized. True, we wished to trade with the Chinese. He had shown how much or how little he desired commerce with us by so carefully hedging about and restricting our interchanges with him at Canton—the single point where they had been permitted to go on at all—that it was as though we received his bales of silk and chests of tea lowered to us from the battlements of an impregnable wall, and delivered our Mexican dollars and British opium to him by the returning rope. Recognition of this extremely attenuated line of commercial intercourse, so far as it existed, was in the form of restrictive rather than encouraging regulations.

It was not that China had any peculiar objection to political and trade relations with America and Europe. She desired no enlargement of her acquaintance in any direction. An imperial decree made any Chinese subject forfeit his head to the executioner, as a punishment for having wandered into foreign parts, if he was so indiscreet as to come within reach of that gentleman by a return to his native land. That law still stands unrepealed, though for many years it has never been enforced. The government order, forbidding the construction of any junks or vessels of a greater length than sixty feet, made all other than short coasting voyages both unprofitable and dangerous. With her ports closed to foreign craft, regardless of nationality, and no domestic vessels fit for even moderately long ocean voyages, it is easy to estimate the extent of China's desire to either receive or return visits from strangers. The sole exception to this exclusion was in favor of a limited number of Siamese merchant-vessels, duly registered and furnished with permits to trade between Bangkok and certain Chinese ports. These made their leisure way northward with the summer or southeastern monsoon, and were blown home again by the northwestern winds of winter, thus making one round voyage each year.

It is unnecessary to the purpose of this volume that the causes which led China to prefer such absolute seclusion should be inquired into and their validity either recognized or denied. That she was totally ignorant of the character and position of Western nations, and necessarily so, is self-evident. It is related that when what is now the German Empire sent commissioners to China to negotiate a treaty, they were refused. On the kindly interference of the British minister, this refusal was withdrawn, the Chinese Government naïvely remarking that it was informed by the British representative that the Germans were really a respectable people, and that their king was a relative of the Queen of Great Britain. For this reason they decided to negotiate a treaty. In 1870 one of the most prominent officials in Peking, being dispatched to Europe upon a special mission, gave directions that some one hundred and fifty pounds of salt should be packed with his other baggage, as he was accustomed to use it in his food, and he had reason to fear difficulty in obtaining it in the regions to which he was bound. A member of the Imperial Cabinet was once overheard, so recently as 1884, inquiring of an associate whether foreigners had any form of marriage contract, or whether the two sexes lived promiscuously together.

Coupled with this unqualified ignorance were certain absurd and amusing notions concerning the habits and personal appearance of the unfortunate creatures who lived beyond the reach of the civilizing influences of the Chinese Empire. The interested student in ethnology may find in the bookstores of Peking and other Chinese cities to-day volumes containing descriptive accounts of some of these outside barbarians, with carefully executed representations of them done in water-colors. One type has ears reaching to the earth, another has no legs worthy of mention. The representation of one tribe forces the student to the conclusion that the Chinese must have heard, and with some accuracy, of the gorilla. One race is pictured as having its face as a sort of boss in low relief upon the breast, while another carries its head conveniently located under the left arm. Small wonder that China desired no close acquaintance with people concerning whom she knew so little and imagined so much.

Prior to this disturbance of her seclusion, China had, for many centuries, been the single central figure in a world largely of her own creation and in which she was the final dominant force. She had been the planet, the powerful civilized, cultivated empire, surrounded by its circle of admiring satellite kingdoms. Corea, upon the northeast, the Mongol families on the north, Kashgar and Samarcand upon the west, Thibet in its Himalayan clouds and snows at the southwest, Burmah and Siam at the south, Annam and Cochin China trailing off from her southeastern border, and the little kingdom of Liu Chiu lying like a fringe in the China Sea—these formed a system, a world, of which the Chinese Empire was the centre. They flattered her by that most delicate and subtle of all forms of flattery, imitation. They copied her forms of civilization, to a considerable extent modeled their governmental systems after hers, borrowed her religions, several of them adopted her written language, gained their knowledge of the arts and literature from her, and all of them deferred and appealed to her as final authority and sovereign mistress of the Oriental world. She was arbiter of their disputes, whether domestic or international. She aided them at times to quell insurrection by force of arms. She held herself and was held as the patron and the superior of all.

In this planetary system—to pursue the figure already used—Japan was the erratic and dangerous comet. Probably no other Oriental nation gained such large and practical advantages from China as did Japan. Her knowledge of art, her written language, much of her literature, at least one of her religious systems, were all borrowed from her great continental neighbor. The very names Japan has given to her two great staple products, tea and silk, show that they were introduced from China. Yet she was always the troublesome neighbor, the one disturbing force in the calm of China's recognized supremacy. Those who imagine that recent troubles between these two nations are exceptional are mistaken. They are but a modern repetition of the history of the past ten centuries.

Between the nations named, excepting Japan and China, a definite and well-understood relationship and intercourse was established. Annual embassies came from the smaller States, at each new year to Peking, bringing presents and the felicitations of the season to the Emperor. They were entertained by him, and on their return home were the bearers of return gifts to the heads of their own nations, which gifts were always as much more valuable than those they brought as the Emperor was greater in power and wealth than their lord. It is only within a very few years that the King of Siam has ceased sending white elephants to the Emperor of China. Some of those sent are still living and kept in the "Elephant Stables" at Peking. And the winter of 1894-95 bids fair to be the first in many decades, if not centuries, in which the King of Corea has failed to dispatch his annual mission to the Chinese capital. Much of the traffic between the two nations was carried on by means of these embassies, a large number of merchants being allowed to accompany them, and the goods they sold and bought being, as a matter of privilege, exempt from duties or imposts of any sort. Whenever the question of succession to the throne became practical in any of these outlying kingdoms, the will of the Emperor of China was taken in case of strife between several claimants. And in some of the States named it had come to be a custom, though never more than a matter of form, for the new incumbent to dispatch a special embassy to Peking to announce his accession and request the gracious recognition of the Emperor. This was peculiarly true of the kings of Corea and Annam.

As might be expected, much confusion and misunderstanding has grown up in the exact and intensely practical Western mind regarding this loose-jointed and essentially Oriental relationship. There is no word in any European tongue which will describe the position which China claims to hold *vis-à-vis* the smaller States named, because the idea is wholly foreign to our notions of international connections. It has therefore, for lack, partly, of a better term, and partly of accurate knowledge of what the relationship was, been spoken of as a suzerainty. Whatever it is, it is not that. The vital point of the connection of suzerain and vassal is that the latter must pay regular sums of tribute and furnish specified military forces to the former. Neither of these has ever been exacted in a single instance. China has repeatedly sent armed bodies of men to assist her weaker neighbors to suppress internal rebellion, but she has never either asked or received aid of that sort from them. And aside from the interchange of New Year gifts, in which China invariably gives more than she receives, there is no such thing as tribute paid by king to emperor.

Vague and indefinite as is this relationship to our minds, it is simple and clear to the Oriental, since it is exactly in the line of his ideas. He describes it as the connection between the elder and the younger brother; and when the Chinese Government has had occasion to mention her position —toward Corea, for example—the same word has been used as is employed to express the relative position in the family of two brothers. Keeping in view the fact that, under the patriarchal system, which is not only in vogue in China, but forms the basis of her entire form of government, the elder brother has a certain authority over and responsibility for the younger, it ceases to be difficult to understand the tie which connects China with her surrounding and less powerful neighbors. It implies a sort of moral authority or right of control, which is entirely foreign to our ideas, and particularly objectionable, since it can be exercised or repudiated at will. And perhaps in the fact that it can be enforced or evaded, as discretion may indicate, is to be found the feature of the system which is most pleasing to the Oriental mind.

It cannot be a matter of surprise to a thoughtful mind that long centuries of unquestioned supremacy, of admiration and flattery from her weaker and less civilized neighbors, had developed an intense national conceit in the Chinese mind, and that she should regard with feelings closely allied to contempt all remote nations which had not been favored with her example, and hence had not formed themselves upon her model. She had her coterie of humble admirers, and desired no questionable additions to the circle. And it must not be forgotten that she had more or less communication with India, and had a substantially correct idea of what European intercourse had meant, from an Oriental standpoint, to that great empire of Southern Asia.

Such being the attitude of China upon the general question of establishing friendly relations with the nations of Europe and America, and such her position of calm, yet absurd, superiority, it was peculiarly unfortunate that acquaintance and association with us was forced upon her in what her government and people could with justice regard as a bad cause.

This is not the place for a discussion of the question whether any nation has the right to insist, by force of arms, if necessary, that any other nation shall establish and maintain commercial and friendly intercourse with it. That question may be left to recognized authorities on international law. Nor is it intended to express an opinion regarding the right or wrong of the so-called opium war. The attempt is here made not to record opinions, but to portray, with some degree of faithfulness and accuracy, a situation. The broad outline of facts is sufficiently well known to all intelligent readers, and each of them can and will draw his own conclusions. But the feeling which those facts aroused in the Chinese, the view which they took of them, and which has very seriously colored their opinions of all foreigners, and influenced the entire course of their foreign relations, are not sufficiently well understood nor its more remote effects always clearly recognized. No true picture of the modern Chinese can be drawn without bringing the opium war upon the canvas. For that reason alone it is introduced.

Whatever may have been the other causes—and they were many and serious—which led to the series of military and naval expeditions against China, from the attack upon the Bogue forts, below Canton, in 1842, to the capture of one of the north gates of Peking and the destruction of the Summer Palace, in 1860, to the Chinese the purpose of all of

these operations is summed up in one word—
opium. He looks upon all other grievances as
pretexts, or as valid only through being made to
subserve one main purpose, the opening of the empire as a vast market for the sale and consumption
of the drug raised in India.

To him the facts are plain and their logic irresistible. There had been much friction between
the authorities at Canton and the agent of the East
India Company for years prior to 1842 over the introduction of the drug into China, either in open
or secret violation of the laws of the empire.
These troubles increased after the expiration of
the charter of the East India Company. They
reached a climax in 1840, when Commissioner Lin
reached Canton, sent there by the Chinese Emperor with the most explicit and peremptory orders
to put a complete end to the opium traffic at all
hazards. He found, shortly after his arrival, opium
on board twenty-two ships in the river below Canton, to the value of about $9,000,000. It was there
in open and notorious violation of the laws of the
empire, and hence was, with the vessels which
brought it, liable, by universally recognized law, to
seizure and confiscation. Its surrender was demanded, and after some peculiar steps taken by
Commissioner Lin to enforce the demand, it was
delivered to him by Captain Elliot, the agent of
the British Government, who also gave a pledge
that no more should be brought into the port.
The opium thus secured (20,291 chests) was at
once completely destroyed by being thrown into
trenches and mixed with lime and salt water, and

this mixture was allowed to run into the river at low tide. Officers were stationed to prevent any one from carrying away any portion of the drug; and one Chinese who endeavored to carry away a small quantity was summarily beheaded. There is not the least reason to doubt that every ounce was disposed of in this thorough manner. These are facts about which there can be no question. The Government of China was honest in its intention to exterminate the opium trade; it was within its right in the demand for the surrender of the contraband drug, and, for once at least, it possessed a servant in Commissioner Lin who inflexibly and thoroughly executed the instructions which he had received.

For this legitimate and praiseworthy act, as the Chinese reason, a British military and naval force was dispatched to China. Several important ports upon the coast were attacked and captured; the Chusan Islands were occupied; Nanking, once the capital of the empire, was besieged, and there China was forced at the point of the bayonet to enter into a treaty with Great Britain by which she agreed to pay $21,000,000. Of this, $6,000,000 was for the opium surrendered and destroyed, $3,000,000 was for other claims, and $12,000,000 for the cost of the war. And the important island of Hong Kong was unconditionally ceded to the Queen.

Such are the facts which the Chinese have in mind, and which give a permanent color to their opinion of foreigners. It is idle to explain other and grave grievances which influenced the action

A GATE OF PEKING.

of the British, and which, had opium never been known, would have demanded forcible interference. They reply by pointing out the fact that these armed operations against their country never fully ceased until the practical occupation of Peking in 1860. The flight of their Emperor and his death in exile had wrung from their government a further concession legalizing the opium traffic in China. Only when that was secured, they say, did Great Britain lay aside her warlike mien and adopt a conciliatory tone and policy. And the efforts made by the Chinese Government—and they have been many and urgent—to induce England to concert measures with China either for the immediate or gradual suppression of the traffic are well known among the more intelligent of the people. It is also well known that these appeals have uniformly been unanswered or refused. This fact lends intensity to their conviction and bitterness to their dislike.

These are the more important features of the situation under which China was dragged from her seclusion, brought face to face with the modern Western world, and forced into new and undesired relationships. That she should resent what, from her standpoint, was an unwarranted intrusion, is but natural. That she should misunderstand and misconstrue the motives of those who were sincerely desirous of serving her best interests was to be expected. Her rulers were in absolute ignorance of both the principles and technicalities of modern international law, and the rules which govern the intercourse of autonomous and equal States.

Through this ignorance they have often put their government in false positions, and hence lost diplomatic battles when the point for which they were striving was right and they ought to have won. They are as well aware of this fact as any of their critics, but are too proud and reserved to openly confess it. One of the members of the Chinese Cabinet said to the author on one occasion: "It makes no difference on which side justice and right lie, whatever the question may be, China is always obliged to take the wall. Even when our case is good, we blunder and lose it." And the pathetic remark contained far more of truth than, perhaps, the speaker himself knew.

Here is an illustration, a case unimportant in itself, yet fully justifying the complaint of the Cabinet minister. It has been the custom in Peking from time immemorial that, whenever the Emperor goes abroad, the streets through which he passes must be closed to public travel. On one such occasion the Chinese Foreign Office, two days in advance of the event, notified the various diplomatic representatives in a courteous note. The streets to be closed were not in that part of the city where foreigners resided; none of them would be in the least incommoded, and, moreover, the interruption to traffic would last only a couple of hours. Yet, with a single exception, every legation in Peking replied, resenting the action of the Chinese authorities. In this case the Chinese Government erred through an excessive desire to be courteous. In no capital of either Europe or America would the municipal authorities, much less the Privy Council of State, trouble themselves to inform foreign ministers of a temporary blockade of certain streets. They would simply close the streets for a day, or a month if need be, and promptly and properly rebuke any question of their action by foreign representatives.

When the Chinese people are more fully understood, their faults, foibles, and virtues recognized —they have many of each—and the history of this first thirty years of intercourse between them and the outside world is accurately written, the wonder will be, not that China has modified her ancient ways so little in this period, but rather that she has changed so much and conformed so largely and, on the whole, so good-naturedly to the demands of modern life. Her people are not stolid, however much they may appear so. But they are naturally cautious, conservative, and intensely proud. They have been rudely awakened from a sleep of centuries—not, it must be admitted, under the most favorable circumstances. And it takes time to safely recast the life and mode of thought of four hundred millions of people.

There is neither force nor point in drawing comparisons between them and the Japanese in regard to their progress in Western civilization. The two races are essentially unlike. Then one more readily casts off borrowed habiliments than those which were originally his own, earned by his labor, and worn until they have become almost an integral part of himself. As has already been pointed out, Japan, in discarding Oriental fashions for Western, was, in the main, merely casting off borrowed

clothing. Those of China, on the contrary, are of
her own devising, and have been slowly and labori-
ously woven as the shuttle of time passed to and
fro through many centuries.

Aside from this, there has been an enormous difference, all in favor of Japan, in both the initiation
and the conduct of their relations with the Western world. Enough has been said of the opium
war which was the occasion of the formal and
forced introduction of China into the so-called
"family of nations." Shortly after that event,
Japan, also at the point of the bayonet, it is true,
received her introduction. The United States performed that ceremony, and made the first treaty.
In both countries there existed rigid laws against
the importation and use of opium. We have seen
how those laws were treated by those who made
the first treaty with China. Our commissioner to
Japan, on the other hand, scrupulously regarded
Japanese legislation and wishes upon this point,
and practically strengthened the determination of
the native authorities. To put the contrast in the
mildest possible form, Great Britain hampered
legislation against the use of opium in China ; the
United States rendered moral support to such
legislation in Japan. The difference between these
two lines of action at the outset is much further-
reaching in its results than is ordinarily supposed.
It is nearly sufficient to account for the different
positions of the two nations to-day. In 1872, Japan
and China then having no treaty relations, a petition was forwarded by certain Chinese residents in
Japan to the United States Legation at Peking,

with the request that it be laid before the Imperial Government. It prayed for the redress of certain serious grievances and hardships to which they were subjected in Japan. The chief complaint was that many of them were opium-smokers, and that the Japanese authorities interfered with their practice of the vice. They summed up their sufferings in this matter with the declaration that the police were even in the habit of entering their sleeping-rooms at night and smelling their breath, in order to discover whether they had been using the opium pipe.

In 1878 the Chinese Government asked the permission of the United States to place certain students, then being educated in this country at its expense, in our military and naval schools at West Point and Annapolis. Although the request was not favorably received, it was earnestly pressed for nearly three years before being abandoned. Our refusal was the main cause of the withdrawal of what was known as the Chinese Educational Mission, the most practical scheme ever undertaken by China for placing herself in line with modern ways and ideas. At the time this request was being urged by China, Japanese students, sent and supported by their government, were learning the art and science of naval warfare at Annapolis, as the Chinese authorities well knew. How far this favor, granted to Japan and refused to China, may have determined the issue of the great naval battle recently fought between the ships of those nations, in which several of the principal Japanese actors were graduates of the United States Naval Academy, cannot, of course, be determined. Nor can it be known how far our refusal disheartened and prejudiced a nation at best only half-hearted in its desire for progress, and timid and uncertain as to the best means of promoting it.

CHINESE OFFICIAL.—MOUNTED.

The United States and all British colonies within a reaching distance of Chinese emigrants, which practically includes all countries in which the Chinese coolie can be certain of the treatment due to human beings, have passed laws against Chinese immigration. No such legislative action has been taken by any against the natives of Japan. While the Chinese Government is decidedly opposed to the emigration of its people, it does not regard them as the scum of the earth, and very naturally objects to discriminative legislation against them.

These comparisons and contrasts are not drawn for the purpose of argument or accusation. The question whether these diverse lines of action toward two neighboring powers, brought out of centuries of isolation about the same time, and each intensely jealous of the other, was wise or unwise, right or wrong, is not raised. They are brought forward solely as facts which have had an essential bearing upon the present attitude and position of China, and hence must be kept in mind by any person who is desirous of obtaining a reasonably accurate conception of the people of that great empire, and the peculiar agencies which have operated, from without as well as from within, to place them where they are to-day.

During the thirty years which have passed since China was opened to the Western world, and brought, without prelude or preparation, face to face with the host of delicate and confusing questions which came with what was really a new national existence, two men have practically shaped the policy and guided the destinies of the empire. When, in 1860, the allied British and French armies reached Peking, Prince Kung, a younger brother of the Emperor, was the only member of the imperial family who remained at the capital. He came forward and made terms of peace with the diplomatic representatives who accompanied the military forces. And from that event until his retirement from office in 1884 he was by far the most conspicuous and influential figure in either the foreign or domestic politics of China. His name is, perhaps, less familiar to foreigners than that of the Viceroy, Li Hung Chang. This arises partly from the fact of his residence at the capital instead of a seaport, and because his imperial rank renders him less democratic and accessible to the ordinary traveler. But for a quarter of a century he was the head and Li Hung Chang the strong right arm of the Chinese Empire.

At the very outset of his public career he successfully initiated a system of diplomatic intercourse with Western powers, established a customs system which has no superior in efficiency, and at the same time crushed out the Taiping rebellion in Central China, and, a little later, the Mohammedan uprising in the northwestern provinces. He satisfied the just indignation of foreign governments at the indescribable horrors of the Tientsin massacre on surprisingly easy terms, fought against and then yielded the audience question when his shrewd foresight showed him that further opposition was dangerous, outwitted Russia in the Kuldja affair, crushed the coolie traffic out of existence, and finally came to grief in connection with the French invasion of Cochin China, though the policy outlined by him in that affair was successfully followed by his successors.

Prince Kung is a past master in the art of Oriental diplomacy. He studies the man pitted against him in any given contest even more carefully than the question at issue. He is overbearing and conciliatory, rude and courteous, frank and reserved, prompt and dilatory, patient and hot-tempered—all exactly as suits his purpose, and with a startling rapidity of change from one *rôle* to another. The great secret of his success lies in his ability to determine in advance when it will be necessary to yield. His sudden changes of front are no indication of a vacillating disposition. They are the shifting of so many masks behind which he studies his opponent, estimates the amount of his determination, and thereby decides his own course. He gives no premonitory sign of surrender, is the more positive and unyielding as the final moment approaches, and then, when his antagonist is bracing himself for a final attack, the enemy suddenly disappears, and a smiling, compliant friend takes his place.

As a leader in what may be termed a defensive foreign policy—and thus far China has had only that—Prince Kung has probably no equal. No man in the empire better understands her future possibilities and present inherent weakness. No man now living there has had any such broad range of experience and responsibility as he. During the twenty-four years of his premiership there was an emperor upon the throne but two, and he was an effeminate and vicious boy, who died from the effects of dissipation. Practically, during his entire term of public service, Prince Kung was the master mind in determining the policy of the government, . and the shrewd and versatile politician and diplomat in its execution. His recent recall to the post formerly held by him is a distinct gain to the empire.

Li Hung Chang was born in the province of An Huei, in Central China, in 1822. He comes from an ordinary Chinese family, which, however, has become noted from the fact that all of the sons in the present generation attained the highest rank in public service, each being entitled to wear the pink coral button. Hence his mother is highly honored among Chinese women. He became prominent in connection with the efforts made by the Imperial Government to suppress the Taiping rebellion, at which time he was governor of one of the provinces which was overrun by the insurgents. He ordered the immediate decapitation of five Wangs, or rebel chiefs, who had surrendered under a pledge made them by General Gordon that their lives should be spared and they should be allowed to go unpunished. He was made Viceroy of Chihli in 1871, and has been retained in that post continuously since. This is the highest viceroyalty in the empire, since the capital is within its limits.

Li has had a large military experience, and in his bearing and modes of thought is more of the soldier than the politician. He is exceptionally large for a Chinese, has a gruff, hearty voice, and is exceedingly democratic in his feelings. Despite the reserve and show of state which is supposed to surround an Oriental of his high station, he is easily reached, and may be seen by any foreigner who can induce his consul to request an interview. Some of these visitors, and they are many, might

LI HUNG CHANG.

learn a lesson in ordinary politeness from the gruff old viceroy. One of them, an ex-governor of one of our States, who had been received with extreme courtesy, remarked to an American friend as they were leaving, the viceroy and his interpreter, through whom the conversation had been conducted, being close at his side, " Well, I don't see that the viceroy is such an old heathen after all."

Throughout his brilliant career, Viceroy Li has given consistent and conclusive evidence of his unswerving fidelity to the reigning family. He has been the strong right arm of the government. To him is mainly due the progress made in building up a navy of modern ships and organizing an army with modern weapons. The Imperial Government has leaned upon him more, relied more upon his counsel, trusted him more implicitly than any other officer, Chinese or Manchu, outside of Peking, within the limits of the empire. And there never has been a time when rumors of disaffection on his part or distrust upon the part of those above him had any foundation in fact. This is not only true of Li Hung Chang, but is equally true of all Chinese officials, so far, at least, as any objection to the reigning dynasty on account of its being Manchu is concerned. Manchu rule has been wise, moderate, and sagacious. Aside from rare cases of personal favoritism, no discrimination whatever is allowed between Chinese and Manchu subjects. The number of Chinese office-holders exceeds enormously the Manchu list. As a matter of fact, the native race has absorbed its conquerors, and the two are practically one. It is as rare to find a Chinese who objects to the Emperor because he is a Manchu, as it is to find one of our British friends objecting to Her Majesty Queen Victoria because of her German extraction.

CHAPTER II.

THE GOVERNMENT OF CHINA.

To misunderstand everything Chinese appears to be the rule in Western lands. And in no direction is this misunderstanding so pardonable, so much, indeed, to be expected, as in questions relating to the government of that empire. To the student of modern political systems, with his ideas of authority based more or less completely upon a popular vote, with its clean-cut and accurate limitations and divisions of power, its immediate and well-defined responsibility to the governed, and its forms and methods carefully exposed to constant publicity, the system which has existed for thousands of years in China appears a hopeless puzzle. To him it is only a confused snarl of undefined and often conflicting power. He searches in vain for the end of the thread by which he may straighten out the tangle, and abandons the task, himself confused and undecided whether the continued existence of such a system, or the fact that any people could be governed by it for a single day, is the more remarkable. He classifies it by that familiar old phrase, an absolute despotism, and, thus labelled, he leaves it.

Such a conclusion, reached from a standpoint exterior to China, is by no means remarkable. Her people possess few or none of those peculiar rights and privileges which appear so essential to others, nor can it truthfully be said that they long for them. Trial by jury is unknown, and the average Chinese defendant would shake his head at the idea, preferring to trust his case to one man rather than to twelve. Like the English and Americans, his language contains no phrase even remotely equivalent to *habeas corpus*. Nor does he know anything about such high-sounding phrases as "the palladium of our rights" and "the *magna charta* of our liberties." He is amused rather than interested at our elections, and has never had any direct voice either in the choice of those who rule over him or in the enactment of legislation. The laws of China are simply the expression of the will of the Emperor, made in individual cases. And the code—for China has a code—is the collection and orderly arrangement of these imperial decrees as they have accumulated through many centuries. They are collated from an immense supply of precedents, and touch every imaginable case and all shadings of circumstance. The Chinese have an invincible repugnance to lawyers. Their strongest objection to all Western modes of judicial procedure is the existence and employment of lawyers in our courts. Said a distinguished Chinese statesman to the author: "We can trust our own judgment and common sense to get at the merits of any case and do substantial justice. We do not need to hire men to prove that right is wrong and wrong right."

The fact is, that while all Western nations are coming more and more closely in their ideas of government to that declaration peculiarly familiar to Americans, that "all governments derive their just powers from the consent of the governed," the Chinese have not yet even considered such a theory. Few of them have heard of it. Their theory, on the other hand, is found, with the change of a single word, in an old book which some of them have seen, and which declares that "the powers that be are ordained of Heaven." They have adhered to this generic idea of authority through all the ages, under emperors good, bad, and indifferent. Through repeated changes of dynasty and thousands of years of time, back to the point where their history ceases to be fact and becomes fanciful legend and myth, they have held unchanged to this idea, and no essential modification can at any period in all the centuries be discovered in their system of government. So far as their records show, it is to-day what it was in the days of Yao and Shun, more than two thousand years ago.

Nor does history record any desire or effort, in all these years, to modify the Chinese form of government. It not only has existed, it has satisfied the people who were ruled by it. It has been copied by smaller adjacent peoples, but never repudiated by its own. It has existed for a far greater period of time than any other system of authority on earth; has ruled an immense multitude of people—probably one third of the population of the globe—and has secured to them a reasonable measure of freedom, peace, and prosperity. It apparently satisfies them as well to-day as it did centuries in the past. There surely must be something good, some element which appeals to the better side of human nature, in any form of power of which this can be said.

ENTRANCE TO THE PALACE.

Whatever may be the explanation, it is not to be found in any lack or deficiency in the Chinese character which would lead the race to submit quietly and without show of resistance to an oppression which other more progressive races would overthrow. The Chinese is cautious, slow, conservative. But he has a sturdy independence of character, an innate and strongly developed love of his rights, and will defend them as promptly and positively as any men elsewhere. He may not select the same methods as others, but he reaches the same end by his own way. The Chinese people have in numberless instances risen in opposition to their local rulers, but it has been an uprising against abuses of the system of government, never against the system itself. They have been known to deal with a local magistrate, such as the mayor of a city, in a most democratic and unceremonious manner ; have gone so far as to pull his queue and slap his face ; but it was not because of the exercise on his part of lawful authority, but because he had exceeded it. They are much given to attaching slang names to their officials, descriptive of their peculiarities of person or administration, and have even called the Emperor by a phrase equivalent to "Our Head Clerk ;" but this last is rare.

Theoretically it may be proper to classify the Chinese system of government as an absolute despotism, but in its practical operations such a description of it not only fails to describe, but is misleading and unjust. It is paternalism pure and simple. Not the man, but the home, the family is the unit of Chinese life. And paternalism, based upon the ancient patriarchal idea of the position and authority of the head of the family, is the theory upon which the form of government is based. The only despotic element in it is to be found in the practically unlimited authority which, under the old patriarchal law, parents exercised over their children. This law is in full force in China to-day, and is perhaps more rigorously enforced than any other. The theory is simple, and may be stated in a single line. The parent is the absolute master of his son, entitled to his service and obedience so long as the parent lives. The son never becomes of age, in our sense of the word, during the life of the father—that is, never becomes independent of him. He must serve him so long as he lives, at the sacrifice of his own wife and children if necessity arise; must honor him with an extravagant funeral at death, mourn him for three years, during which period his wife must not give birth to a child, and offer sacrifice twice each year, so long as he himself lives, at his father's tomb.

The Chinese code provides that any one who is guilty of addressing abusive language to his or her father or mother, or father's parents, or a wife who rails at her husband's parents or grandparents, shall be strangled. Other penalties equally severe are provided for all possible offences against filial duty. And no statutes in the empire are more rigorously enforced. Upon the other hand, the father, having been given uncontrolled authority over his son throughout his life, is held responsible by the government for the conduct of the son. If the latter violates any law, his parents and grandparents, if living, are punished with him, upon the theory that they had failed in their duty to instruct him in such a way as to make him a good citizen. A most shocking illustration of this theory occurred in Peking in 1873. A Chinese was convicted of having broken open the tomb of a prince and robbed the coffin of some valuable ornaments contained within it. Although there was no evidence to show that any relative of his was aware of the crime, much less a party to it, yet the entire family of thirteen persons, representing five generations, and including a man more than ninety years of age and a babe of less than two months, were put to death. The criminal and his parents were sliced in pieces; of the others, the men were beheaded and the women strangled.

It is necessary to keep carefully in mind this patriarchal idea of parental authority, since from it the entire system of government in China has developed. The family is the microcosm which, enlarged but otherwise unchanged, forms the type of power throughout the empire. The family, with its autocratic head, is the unit. Next comes the simplest form of combination in the village life, in which is found a considerable degree of local self-government, the old men being allowed a certain control, and being in return held responsible for the good conduct and proper discipline of the younger. Practically this semi-official council of elders is allowed to regulate the less important affairs of the commune without interference, and its opinion has great weight in the adjustment of questions of more gravity. Its functions have been fully recognized, not merely by high officials, but by every emperor who has occupied the throne. Some two hundred years ago the Emperor Kang Hsi, one of the wisest in the long list, prepared a series of eighteen essays upon the varied duties of his subjects in all their relations to each other and the State, and the elders in the different villages throughout the empire were commanded to call all the young men together upon the 1st and 15th of each month and to read and expound to them the whole or a part of one of these essays. Following the village group comes naturally the larger combinations up to the province, which corresponds substantially with our State. And these, eighteen in number in China proper, form the empire.

The central figure in this system is, of course, the Emperor. He is the sire, the father of all the Sons of Han, as the Chinese are proud to call themselves. He receives his authority direct from Heaven. He is the source of law and the fountainhead of authority, the owner by Divine right of every foot of land and every dollar's worth of property in the empire. China has no domestic debt, and under this system can have none, for when the Emperor needs what is his and is still nominally in the possession of his subjects, he does not borrow, he simply takes it. All the forces and wealth of the empire are his, and he may claim the services of all male subjects between the ages of sixteen and sixty. He has another, a sacerdotal function, which adds largely to the reverence and semi-sacred character in which he is held by the people, and to which is due the seclusion in which he is kept. He is the son of Heaven, and, as such, Heaven's highpriest. He alone can worship and offer sacrifice on behalf of his people at the great altar of Heaven. In this service he has no recognized substitute or subordinate. He stands alone between his people and the Heaven which is to them the final power, the source of blessing and bane, the sentient and perfect judge, swift to reward virtue and punish vice. But he stands there as its son and servant, thus forming the connecting link between his chil-

VIEW OF PEKING.

dren and Heaven, which is, in their eyes, his ancestor and theirs.

While the imperial power thus described appears to be absolutely without limit, it is, in point of fact, no more despotic or arbitrary than that with which the head of every family in China is clothed. It is precisely the same in both kind and degree. The Emperor is simply the patriarch of his people. He exercises in that great area which forms the nation, and which they call "The Central Empire," neither more nor less than the same powers and privileges which each father of a family, even the meanest and most ignorant, exercises in his mud-walled and straw-thatched hovel. He delegates his parental authority, of necessity, to officers of various ranks and degrees, and each of them becomes by this act the father of those under his jurisdiction. The patriarchal idea is the vital cord, the generic theory of the entire system; and in that fact is to be found the explanation of its permanence and the power which it has among the people.

To these officers is given so large a measure of discretionary power that, in a considerable degree, each district becomes, like the village, self-governing. Practically officials are held responsible for certain results. Ways and means are left to their judgment. They must keep order and administer justice within their jurisdiction to such an extent at least that no complaints are lodged against them at Peking, and collect and remit the amount of taxes due to the central government. The imperial commands appear not to run beyond those points. The results of this freedom of action are twofold. They give, as has been stated, a considerable degree of liberty to local authorities to consult the popular will, and while they permit a vicious official to abuse his position, they make it certain that the popular censure for maladministration shall rest upon him and not upon the source of his power. The government is thus loose-jointed in its application rather than the reverse; and when the people complain, which they are not slow to do if occasion arise, it is not of despotic interference with their affairs, but of indifference, not of too much government, but of too little. He who has absolute authority seldom exercises any. The despot is a mere figure-head, a nonentity.

It must also be said that the laws, as a whole, are mild and humane, far superior to those found in any other Asiatic country. Sir George Stanton, who translated the Chinese code, said of it: "When we turn from the ravings of the Zend-Avesta or the Puranas to the tone of sense and business in this Chinese collection, it is like passing from darkness to light, from the dwellings of dotage to the exercise of an improved understanding; and redundant and minute as these laws are in many particulars, we scarcely know a European code that is at once so copious and so consistent, or is nearly so freed from intricacy, bigotry, and fiction."

There are a variety of other causes tending to promote the complacency of the people with their rulers and the form of government under which they live. There are numerous checks and guards against abuse of power. The path of appeal to Peking lies always open; and, theoretically at least, it can be traveled without money and without price. Although the Imperial Government seldom shows its hand in interference with the local authority, it has a complete system of espionage over all of its subordinates. One of the departments at the capital is charged with the duty of keeping a record of the conduct of every officer in the empire.

Aside from the more serious rewards and penalties of promotion or dismissal, a record similar to the credit and demerit system of school days is kept, and the balance tells for or against the career of the given officer, as the case may be. Some of these entries are whimsical in their nature when viewed from a Western standpoint, especially as it is common for officials, even of the highest rank, to report themselves for punishment, and because of events which were manifestly beyond their control. That celebrated warrior and statesman, Li Hung Chang, has more than once petitioned the Emperor that a punishment might be awarded him because a river within his jurisdiction had overflowed its banks, owing to excessive rain. Another, only less distinguished than he, asked to be removed from office because a drought and consequent famine had come upon the people of the province which he governed, presumably through some fault of his.

The central government has also a series of rewards for especial diligence and ability in public service. A peacock feather to be worn in the official hat, and possessed of no eye or of one, two, or three eyes, according to the magnitude of the favor shown, is one of these. Another is the permission to enter the outer gate of the palace on horseback. Another is a sable robe. And the last and most prized of all is a short jacket of imperial yellow, the color sacred to His Majesty. These personal marks of favor may be given or withdrawn without interfering with the actual position of him who gains or loses them. The last two named are bestowed only upon officials of the highest rank. Titular honors are also at times bestowed upon the deceased ancestors of praiseworthy servants of the government—a well-meant but useless reward to them for having given to the service of the Emperor zealous and devoted sons.

The two most important factors in securing the permanence of the Chinese governmental system, and winning for it throughout the centuries the continued and hearty support of all classes of the people, remain to be noticed.

The system has been described as pure paternalism, based upon the patriarchal idea of authority. The student of the system may hold either of two opinions. He may regard the form of government as the natural outgrowth of the peculiar genius or bent of the Chinese mind, or he may look upon it as arbitrarily adopted in the early ages of the human race, and ascribe its perpetuity to a long-continued system of education, which has so shaped the popular mind as to conform it to the fundamental idea of government. With either view the result is the same. The Chinese Empire stands solidly imbedded in the minds of the people. It satisfies both their judgment and affections. Their idea and range of instruction have remained unchanged for more than twenty centuries, and filial piety is by far the most essential duty taught in it. That virtue is held as the source and root of all goodness, as the mainspring of morality, and the fountain-head of all honor and prosperity.

Filial piety may properly be styled the only original religion of the Chinese. It is taught in every text-book of every school, and from the beginning to the end of the educational course. Exceptional examples of the practice of the virtue have been in all past time and are now brought to the notice of the Emperor, and by him rewarded with exceptional honors. Every boy and girl in the empire has, as a part of necessary education, been told the stories of certain Chinese who practiced this duty in a remarkable degree. Their names and the manner in which their devotion to their parents was shown are fresh in the minds of every person in the empire. There are twenty-four of these renowned and special exhibitions. The " Sacred Edicts of the Emperor Kang Hsi," already mentioned, contains one chapter devoted to exhortation to the practice of this virtue ; and one incident is given illustrative of the beneficial effects of its exercise not included in the twenty-four, and so peculiar as to be well worthy of translation. It runs as follows : " There was also in the district of Chiang Cho a single family named Ch'ên, comprising, in its various generations, more than seven hundred persons, all of whom ate at one table.

Among them they possessed some one hundred and fifteen or one hundred and twenty dogs, who also ate their food together. If any one of the dogs failed to come to his food, none of the others would consent to eat." "You see," moralizes the venerable and wise Emperor, "this Ch'ên family,

CHINESE RIVER SCENE.

by their concord and harmonious lives, had converted and regenerated all of their dogs."

It is, perhaps, unnecessary to inquire whether "this Ch'ên family" possessed a peculiar breed of dogs, or whether the Emperor had been imposed upon. The tale serves fitly to illustrate the variety of ways and means by which this duty of filial obedience is impressed upon the minds of the people, until the phrase has become with them a synonym for the sum of all virtue and the climax of all religion. Confucius found this idea already existent, and he so enforced and embodied it in his code of political ethics as to immeasurably increase its power. To him it was alike the root and culmination of all private or national virtue and wisdom. His writings have shaped the minds of the people and the policy of the empire for more than two thousand years. He is quoted alike by prince and peasant, by emperor and beggar. A quotation from Confucius has settled many a quarrel, arbitrated many a dispute. And, beyond question, this long-continued and consistent line of education, coincident at every point with the root idea of the governmental system, has had an immense effect in giving permanence to that system, and in the control of the people under it.

The other important element in the conservation of the system is found in the fact that the administrators of the affairs of state are chosen from among the people themselves. The imperial family, aside from its head, has never absorbed many of the offices nor concerned itself with the government. There is no titled nobility, with its long list of elder and younger sons, sons-in-law, and cousins near and remote, to be supported from the public funds and to fill all the more important positions of honor and profit. The few titles that are from time to time bestowed carry nothing with them but the nominal honor; they are bestowed as rewards for distinguished services, and have never been recognized as forming the basis of any claim whatever upon either offices or treasury. In a way they are hereditary, but soon run out, since the rank decreases one grade with each generation. Even the imperial clan forms no exception to this rule. The author has many a time had in his employ a man who, as a blood relative of the Emperor, was entitled to wear the imperial yellow girdle ; but he was a hod-carrier, and earned six cents a day.

There is thus no class or barrier of persons entitled to special privileges between the Emperor and his people. Succession to the throne itself, while it is practically a matter of hereditary descent, is not necessarily so. The eldest son is not the heir apparent. The Emperor names his successor, and is supposed to study the character of all his sons and to select that one who is, in his judgment, best qualified to manage the affairs of state. The eldest is frequently put aside ; and one of the best rulers of the present dynasty was the fourteenth son of his father. Theoretically the Emperor may go entirely outside his own family, and select his successor from among any family of his subjects. This course, however, is never followed.

Here, then, is seen at a glance the Chinese system. The Emperor stands alone. He is the son of Heaven, the father of the empire, with its countless millions of population. The innumerable " hands and eyes of the throne," his officers of every grade of degree, rank, and responsibility are chosen, under a carefully devised series of regulations, from among the people themselves. The door to office is open to all. Every boy in the empire is a possible prime-minister. But each one must start at the bottom of the official ladder, and the height to which he may climb is then determined solely by his own ability, zeal, and fidelity. This is not a mere theory, it is a fact. The majority of the high ministers of state in China who have held office during the past centuries, and hence whose histories can readily be traced, began life as poor boys—poor with a poverty of which we fortunately know nothing. To name one or two by way of example merely: Wên Hsiang, one of the greatest Chinese statesmen of the present dynasty, and for many years prime-minister, was the son of a farmer, who reared a large family upon less than ten acres of leased land. His colleague and successor, Shen Kuei Fên, was the son of a street peddler, who esteemed himself fortunate if he made a profit of ten cents a day from his business. Such cases are not exceptions; they form the rule.

Leaving out of sight the mode of selection, the fact that officials in China are not chosen by the people, but named by the Emperor, there is a remarkable similarity between the system in vogue in that great Oriental empire and that followed by the United States. There, as here, it is a government of the people by officers chosen from among the people, with no bar to the ambition of any of the governed to become a governor. And the result is much as might be expected. There is intense ambition to fill positions which are universally recognized as belonging to the people, a sturdy freedom and independence of opinion in the criticism of the conduct of magistrates, and a general spirit of democracy in the popular mind which forms the most remarkable anomaly to those who, not having the key to the puzzle, look upon the administration of Chinese affairs as a type of pure despotism. Perhaps no better proof of the fact that all classes of the people fully understand the theory and practice upon which the government is based can be found than the marked difference of manner with which they speak of their officials, even the highest, and of the Emperor. Of the former they speak with the utmost freedom ; criticise their public acts and private life, dub them with nicknames, and generally treat them as their own fellows. Of the Emperor they speak with bated breath, and only in the most reverential accents.

It is not easy to overestimate the power which such a governmental system has to consolidate and perpetuate itself in the affections of the governed. Laxity of administration or its extreme opposite, tyrannous oppression, are alike condoned, as being the fault of the particular incumbent of office rather than of the system. Every family in the empire has or aims to have a relative, more or less remote, in some grade of public service, and hence extortion, perversion of justice, and all the long list of possible wrongs are borne with a patience and complacency which could not endure for a moment if the official class were not chosen from or did not constitute a part of the people themselves.

This mode of selection of the administrators of public affairs, described more in detail in another chapter, has a tremendous power in conserving and perpetuating the government of China.

CHAPTER III.

THE LANGUAGE.

It is impossible to know any people well until the student can speak and think in their tongue. And a barrier far more serious than the Great Wall to any intimate acquaintance with the Chinese is found in their language. It is the oldest spoken language now existent upon the earth, has been the mother tongue of a far larger number of human beings than any other either in the past or present, and, so far as can be determined, has undergone no serious changes either in its construction or written form since it came into existence. It has had, in common with all other languages, a constant process of growth and decay; new ideas have required new symbols of expression. Characters have dropped out of common use as the ideas which they represented were lost or modified. But the national habit of thrift and economy appears to have shown itself even in their word-building. While new characters have been added to the language, none of the old ones have been absolutely dropped. The result is an enormous list of words, which literally "no man can number." The estimate of the total number of distinct characters in the Chinese language ranges all the way from 25,000 to 260,000. The Kang Hsi Tz Tien—the standard dictionary of China—contains 44,449. Probably not more than 10,000 of these are in constant use even among the educated classes. The nine volumes of the Chinese classics contain only 4601 different characters, though in five of the nine volumes are found a total of over two hundred thousand words. Hence the list of what we would call obsolete characters must be far more extensive than that of the active living characters of the language. But pedantry, as shown in searching for and making use of some long-forgotten character, is a virtue among the Chinese, and one of the favorite modes of exhibiting great scholarship is by interlarding a memorial to the throne, or an essay, with a host of characters resurrected from the most ancient *débris* of the language. While this enormously increases the labor of learning Chinese—makes it, indeed, an endless task—it carries with it one comfort. It is no discredit to any person, however learned, to be ignorant of the form, sound, or meaning of characters met in his daily reading.

The Chinese language has no alphabet. Each character represents in itself a complete idea, and hence it is spoken of as a monosyllabic language. But, practically speaking, each character corresponds more nearly to our syllable. As ordinarily used, it is no more nearly monosyllabic than is English. It is written in columns from top to bottom of the page, and from right to left. A Chinese book ends where ours begins. Writing is done

A LOCK ON THE GRAND CANAL.

with a fine camel's-hair brush and india ink. The
process of printing in China, known centuries before the discovery of the art in Europe, is very simple. A leaf of the manuscript, written exactly as it
is to be printed, page for page, is pasted upon a
block of wood. The "block-cutter" chisels out
the entire surface of the block to a slight depth
except that covered by the lines of the characters.
The surface thus prepared is brushed over with ink,
a sheet of paper is laid upon it and pressed gently
and then removed. The book is thus printed, a
page at a time. Volumes in the handwriting of
the author are not unusual. But literary gentlemen among the Chinese are not exempt from the
habit of bad penmanship common to their class in
other lands, and, as a rule, the manuscript is generally rewritten by an expert scribe.

The lack of any alphabet and the enormous number of characters make the labor of learning to
read Chinese burdensome in the extreme. Each
character must be learned by itself, and when the
student has mastered a thousand or five thousand,
the succeeding thousands must be learned in the
same way. Those already familiar furnish no other
assistance than a certain quickness to perceive the
peculiar form which serves to distinguish each
from its fellows. But there is a peculiar fascination in the study of these same characters when
once they are known. The student of any foreign
tongue learns more than how to think and speak
in it. He may learn much of the range of ideas
and standard of judgment of the people who use
it. Each word is a photograph, more or less exact,

of the conception which those who use the word have of the idea which they intend it to express.

This is peculiarly true of the written language of China. In their original forms the characters were rude outlines of the objects they were intended to represent. The first change to which they were subjected was the omission of unimportant lines, leaving only such parts of the picture as represented the peculiar form or essential points of the object. Thus a man was represented with an upright line for the body and two spreading lines for legs; a sheep, by lines so drawn as to represent the horns, head, feet, and tail; cattle, by a head, two horns, and a tail; the sun, by a circle with a dot in the centre; and a tree, by lines representing the trunk, roots, and branches. In this way a limited number of forms, to indicate single visible objects, were secured.

Next came the combination of these simple outlines to represent ideas rather than objects. And the study of this process of word-building is especially fascinating, since a large proportion of the compounded characters are, of necessity, ideographic. Dissect one of them and there lies before you, in its component parts, the Chinese conception of the elements which combine to form the idea which the character represents. Those ancient Chinese word-builders crystallized into these combinations their own conceptions, often crude, inadequate, and even grotesque, of the ideas which they sought to express. Here are a few of these combinations by way of illustration: Two trees represent a forest, three a thicket. The sun beside the moon represents brightness. A prisoner is literally a man in a box. A mouth in a door signifies to ask; a mouth and a dog, to bark; and a woman watching at a window, jealousy. A pig under a roof indicates the Chinese idea of home, and a woman beside a pig under a roof, the marriage of a woman; while the character "to seize" placed over a woman shows the Celestial idea of the part played by a man in a matrimonial alliance. And when a Chinaman made a woman placed beside a broom represent a wife, he painted thereby his own conception of her principal office in the family. On the other hand, he gave an illustration of his love for male offspring when he made a woman standing beside a son signify good. He indicates his modest conception of wealth, since his combination consists of one mouth under a roof and over a field. Other and perhaps more natural compounds, from our standpoint, are "white" and "heart," to signify fear; a hand beside a man meaning to help, and a man standing by words as a symbol of faith. Few would fail to recognize the aptness of thought under a tiger as a symbol for worry or care, or heart beside a pig-sty as signifying mortification or disgrace. But we have a sorry picture of Chinese ideas of womankind in their representation of peace or rest by one woman under a roof, while two women mean "to quarrel," and three together signify intrigue of the most disgraceful kind. Generally speaking, the frequent use of the character meaning woman in combinations in which the idea to be expressed is wrong in its nature more than adequately illustrates the ancient Chinese idea that the female sex is "moulded out of faults." These Orientals have both antedated and gone further than the French, who, when a man is found guilty of offence, ask: "Who is the woman?" They have woven the idea into the very fabric of their language. They show their relationship to Adam by pointing, like him, to the woman as the chief source of temptation and sin.

In the construction of phrases and idiomatic expressions a similar peculiarity exists. Their idioms are by turns simple, quaint, grotesque, full of force, and utterly devoid of any apparent connection with the idea they represent. By way of example, they show a peculiarly low national idea of the color white by its general use to signify uselessness or failure. A "white man" means a useless good-for-nothing, while a "red man" is a popular, successful person. A "white house" is a hovel; "white talk" means unsuccessful argument, and "white running" means labor spent in vain. As the language in common use is practically a hopeless entanglement of these phrases and idioms, from most of which time has stripped all their original force and connection, it will readily be seen that the task of becoming familiar with an innumerable list of characters is, after all, less difficult than that of building them into sentences which, from a Chinese standpoint, shall be intelligible and correct. More foreigners fail to speak idiomatic Chinese than to acquire a reasonable knowledge of the written characters. And the failure is far more serious.

Fortunately the grammar of the language gives no trouble. It is so simple as to be almost non-existent. The words appear to have been worn smooth and round by long use, and may be used for the different parts of speech almost at will. The same word serves indifferently as a noun, verb, adverb, or adjective, or for any other subordinate purpose as may please the speaker. Moods, tenses, persons, gender, and number are all lacking. Conjugations, declensions, and the whole tribe of auxiliary verbs are conspicuous only by their absence. A single character furnishes the root-idea. All qualifications of it must be effected by the addition of other characters. The few educated Chinese who have made any attempt to master the English tongue look with horror and amazement upon what they regard as the clumsy grammatical construction of our language. And it must be confessed that while it furnishes many a pitfall to the unwary speaker to whom it is his mother tongue, it becomes a hopeless task to the foreigner.

A distinguished Chinese official, who had once made a sea voyage with the author of this volume, presented him with a fan as a pleasant souvenir of their companionship in travel. He was a celebrated scholar among his own people, an indefatigable student, and while in mourning for the death of his father, and consequent retirement from office, had, without a teacher, and with no other aids than a Bible, Webster's Dictionary, a copy of Watts and Select Hymns, and some "copy-books," spent nearly three years in the effort to learn English. The accompanying reproduction of a photograph of the fan shows in part how well he had succeeded. Every stroke seen in the picture was done by him with an ordinary Chinese

SOUVENIR FAN.

brush, the English text as well as the native. The latter is elegant both in poetic style (it is a poem) and in penmanship; and the writing of the English translation is marvelous when the implement used is remembered. In " the black ocean" the marquis referred to a fog at sea which had much alarmed him ; the " red" water was the muddy current at the river's mouth which marked the end of the voyage. The " captain's bed" was a sofa upon which the donor of the fan and the author spent many hours in conversation. It was in the captain's cabin, which was occupied by the author during the voyage. There is a certain odd division of words and lameness of grammar in the English text, which is, however, an accurate reproduction of the main idea of the original Chinese.

In another effort this distinguished scholar was less fortunate. He fell into the bog of our auxiliary verbs, and never came to land. Here is his English version of a poem, written also upon a fan, in praise of the scholarship of an American friend. The Chinese text was not less elegant than that shown above :

" To combine the reason of heaven, earth and man,
Only the sage's disciple who is can.
Universe to be included in knowledge all men are should,
But only the wise man who is could.
I have heard doctor enough to have compiled the branches of science
And the books of Chinese and foreigners all to be experience.
Chosen the deeply learning to be deliberated are at right.
Take off the jewels by side of the dragon it as your might."

As has been shown, Chinese characters are, to a large extent, mental pictures of the ideas which they are intended to express. They hint at the thought, but give no clew to the sound or pronunciation. There is absolutely nothing about a Chinese character that will give the perplexed student even a faint hint as to how it shall be uttered by the voice. And this is a generic point of difference between the written language of China and those of America and Europe. There, characters paint the idea; the use of it in speech must be learned separately. Here the word, or combination of letters, is more of a guide to correct pronunciation than to the thought of which it is supposed to be the sign.

While the Chinese tongue discloses various lines of thought, delicate turns of speech, and, so to speak, accurate shades of idea unknown in English, there are many subjects in which the language is totally devoid of words, many ideas for which there are no forms of expression, simply because those ideas have never entered the Chinese head. In the whole range of scientific language, for example, and the simpler terms and phrases used in our text-books in common schools, no equivalent expressions are found in Chinese, because the sciences and even the simpler studies are unknown to them.

By direction of the Secretary of State, the author once addressed a dispatch to the Chinese Foreign Office, which is composed of the entire Cabinet, requesting that certain facilities be extended to several naval officers who were instructed to take observations in order to determine a magnetic secondary meridian of longitude. No reply was received to the request for a week, and then came a note saying that the Prince Regent

and the Cabinet would call the next afternoon to
inquire after the author's health. They arrived at
the appointed hour, and having shown anxious
solicitude for the physical welfare of their host,
who had not been ill a day during the ten or more
years of their acquaintance with him, the real object of their visit came to light. They introduced
it by the most profuse and extravagant compliments for the elegant diction and high literary style
of the dispatch. It was chaste, clean cut, and
exact. No native scholars in modern days could
write better Chinese ; but—and here they hesitated and commented upon their own stupidity and
ignorance—they had not the most remote idea
what it meant. They could gather that the dispatch made a request, but beyond that point they
groped in utter darkness. An hour of explanation,
while it manifestly failed to give them any clear
idea of the nature of a secondary meridian of longitude, showed them that the request involved nothing dangerous or that would be unwise to grant.
They naïvely admitted that the Cabinet had been
for a week divided regarding the contents of the
dispatch ; one faction, headed by the Secretary of
the Treasury, insisting that it referred to a quarantine, since it contained one character used in connection with cholera, while the others followed
the lead of the Prince Regent, who held that it had
something to say about a dynamite gun. The day
following this visit a most courteous reply was received granting the request.

But, after all, the difficulties, already described,
which confront any person who would become

familiar with the Chinese language as a necessary preliminary to acquaintance with the Chinese people, are not insurmountable. Patience, an accurate eye, and a retentive memory will enable any person to learn a sufficient number of characters for practical every-day use. And that is as far as it would be necessary to go. Few foreigners care to become finished scholars in this ancient, interesting language. Even the more perplexing idioms may be mastered if patience in committing them to memory and judgment in their use do not fail.

The really serious difficulties inherent in the Chinese language, and which render it an almost insurmountable barrier to any thorough knowledge of the people, lie in the use of the language in conversation. No amount of book study will enable a person to speak it. It must be learned from the lips of a living teacher. With any amount of drill it requires a quick ear and great flexibility of the vocal organs to acquire accurate pronunciation. So serious is the difficulty, that it may be accepted as a rule that no person over thirty years of age can learn to speak Chinese correctly, as the vocal organs, after that period, appear to have lost a portion of their flexibility. Many persons under that age fail to acquire a command of the language even with the most faithful effort. Not one foreign speaker of Chinese in ten can make the ordinary Chinese cat call. Although I accomplished this feat, I failed, after seventeen years of patient effort, to produce a certain sound with which the donkey-driver urges his long-eared beast about the streets of Peking. My only consolation in the failure is that no other foreigner has been known to master it.

There is little use in the attempt to reduce the sounds to writing. Leaving out of sight the fact that one broad peculiarity which affects every word in the language, and which is yet to be described, could not be covered by any system of reduction, no alphabet or combination of alphabets has been found which will accurately represent the sounds. And, as will readily be seen, to follow a representation that was only approximately correct, no matter how close the approximation, would cause the student always to speak with a brogue. As a rule, the vowel sounds are simple and easy. The consonants are peculiar, and some of them almost beyond the reach of the vocal organs of foreigners.

The best—that is, the most expert foreign authorities—disagree as to the best approximate representation in letters of any alphabet of many of these sounds. It probably will never be settled whether the Chinese word for "man" should begin with *j* or *r*; the fact being that the exact sound is an intermediate one, almost impossible to any foreigner, between the two. The writer once asked each of several American and European scholars learned in the Chinese language, who were guests at his table, how the Chinese word meaning "porridge" should be represented with English letters. He received the following replies: "*Chou*," "*chow*," "*cheu*," "*chau*," "*tcheau*," "*djou*," and "*tseau*." In like manner, the word for "fowl" is transliterated by different Anglo-

Chinese authorities in the following manner: "*Chi*," "*ki*," "*dji*," "*kyi*," and "*tsi*." And all of these different modes of representation refer to the common, plain hen.

The Chinese, curious in their language as in everything else, seem unable to catch the differences between our liquid sounds represented by *l*, *m*, *n*, and *r*. They confuse and misplace them in their efforts to speak English. Yet each of these sounds is constantly and correctly used by them in their native tongue. There is a large class of Chinese words having an initial sound fairly represented by *sh* as initial, and another, smaller but numerous, which must be represented by those letters reversed, or *hs*, as the initial sound.

Again, all words which, if spelled in English letters, would begin with *ch*, *p*, and *t*, are subdivided into two classes. There is an *aspirated ch*, *p*, and *t*, and an *unaspirated ch*, *p*, and *t*. If by mistake one aspirates an initial *t* where it ought not to be aspirated, or the reverse, he, by that error, changes entirely the meaning of the word spoken. Thus, "*tan*," the *t* being unaspirated, means an egg, and exactly the same sound with an aspirated *t* means charcoal. The writer once heard a venerable missionary address the Deity in prayer before a crowded Chinese audience as "O Thou Omniverous God." He meant to say "omniscient," but used an aspirated *ch* when the other would have better served his purpose. On another occasion a missionary saw with astonishment an audience hurriedly leave his chapel in response to what he supposed was a courteous invitation from his lips to them to be seated. In point of fact, however, he was not giving them a welcome, but assuring them that they had made a mistake in entering. An aspirated *t* caused all the misunderstanding. While it is true that an unaspirated *ch*, *p*, and *t* represent very closely the same sounds as *g*, *b*, and *d*, they still are not exactly the same. Any attempt to use those sounds, while they would doubtless enable the speaker to be understood, would at the same time effectually prevent him from speaking accurate Chinese. And this fact fitly illustrates the exceedingly delicate gradations of some of the sounds in the language.

Another broad peculiarity, which affects every word spoken in Chinese, and forbids all attempt at reduction to alphabetical form, remains to be noticed. In English and most other tongues the sound of what is called a word conveys a single and invariable idea to the person to whom it is spoken. The tone in which the word is uttered may serve to indicate inquiry, contempt, sarcasm, surprise, anger, or any other emotion; but the fundamental, the root idea, as we may call it, which is conveyed by the sound remains always the same. Thus in our tongue a man is always a man, whether the word is uttered with sudden explosive force, as in anger, with rising inflection, as in inquiry, or with any other variety of intonation.

All this is changed in Chinese. Here the tone of utterance affects, or rather determines, the root idea as much as the sound itself does. The tone is equal partner with the sound in fixing the idea to be conveyed; and any error in the one is as fatal to the correct expression of any thought intended to be conveyed by the speaker as an error in the other. In Chinese a man ceases to be a man the instant you change the tone of your voice in uttering the word. He may be a disease, a nightingale,

TOAD CATCHING FLIES.

(*From Chinese Painting.*)

or a carrot, but he can be a man in only one tone of voice.

In the standard or mandarin dialect, as it is called among foreigners, there are four of these tones or inflections of the voice: first, a high-keyed, explosive tone ; second, a rising tone, as in asking a question with us ; third, a curving inflection ; and fourth, a falling inflection. A sound uttered in one of these tones has a meaning devoid of all relationship to or connection with exactly the same sound uttered in either one of the other three. Thus, to take the sound " man" again, if uttered in the first tone, it means brazen-faced ; in the second tone, to hide ; in the third, full ; and in the fourth, slow. Another sound which might be represented by our word " one," if used in the first tone, means warm ; in the second, educated ; in the third, steady ; and in the fourth, to ask.

These illustrations show fully that there is absolutely no connection in idea between the different tones of the same sound. They show also that the tone is equal partner with the sound in fixing the meaning of any utterance. Perhaps no rule of English speech is responsible for so many blunders in Chinese as that which requires the rising inflection to be given to the final word of a question which can be answered by " yes" or " no." The obedience to this rule becomes instinctive ; it pursues the unhappy foreigner into his Chinese, where, instead of indicating a question, it fatally affects the meaning of the last word of his sentence, and plays havoc generally with what he would say. He is fortunate if it renders his remark nonsensical rather than insulting.

With peculiarities of consonant sounds unknown in any Western tongue, and with a special tone to each idea, a mistake in which changes the entire meaning, it is no easy matter to speak a single word of Chinese correctly. A long and steady drill of the vocal organs is necessary to the accurate and ready pronunciation of each separate character. At the outset of his Chinese studies the author devoted four hours each day for eight weary months to a drill on the tone table—a table in which each sound in the language is given in the four different tones—and for many months afterward had occasional reviews of it.

There are as many variations in these tones for the sake of rhythm as there are exceptions to some rules of English grammar—variations which add greatly to the labor of the student. Thus, for example, if, in any word of two syllables or sounds, the second is the emphatic syllable and is of the fourth tone, the tone is changed to the first. But the presence of so many varying inflections in Chinese gives a rhythmic swing to the language which makes it pleasant to speak and exceedingly grateful to the ear. With some speakers whose inflections are clear-cut and accurate, it sounds much like chanting. One might expect this effect, since it is impossible to speak in a monotone, and the voice, in any sentence, must pass through five notes of the musical scale.

But the pleasure of Chinese speech comes, if at all, as a well-earned reward for indomitable perseverance in mastering the most difficult language on earth, and is interrupted, often in the study and not seldom afterward, by the most annoying and absurd blunders. A volume might be filled with them. A missionary once informed his audience that the Saviour, when on earth, " went about eating cake." He intended to say "healing the sick;" but an aspirate wrongly placed changed healing into eating, while an error in tone made cakes out of those who were ill.

Upon one occasion, when the writer sat at his dinner-table as the host of a large party, he called the attention of his Chinese butler to some little item that was lacking from the table, and directed him to supply it. The butler appeared puzzled, asked if the article named was desired, and on being assured that it was, and must be produced at once and without more words, disappeared, and in a moment returned, bringing upon a tray, and with that wonderful gravity which never deserts a well-trained Chinese servant, the kitchen poker—an iron rod some three feet in length, knobbed at one end and sharpened to a point at the other. He probably believed that the host was about to brain one of his guests; but that was none of his business, and the poker was gravely presented to his master, who had simply placed an aspirate where it did not belong.

Upon another occasion my cook was directed to arrange, upon short notice, for a large evening reception. In order to lighten his labors, he was told that he might purchase one hundred "ladies' fingers" at the confectioner's. About two hours after this order was given he entered the legation riding upon the shaft of a Chinese cart, dismounted, entered the office, and reported that he had thoroughly searched that section of Peking, but had been able to buy only sixty-four "ladies' fingers." It would be necessary to go to a distance to secure the remaining thirty-six. He was told that the number bought would answer, and then asked why he had hired a cart. "To bring them home," he replied. "But could you not bring them?" was the next question. To this he replied : "Of course not; they weigh five or six pounds each." An immediate inspection of that cart was the sequence of this startling statement regarding tiny strips of cake to be served with ice cream, with the result that the master found himself the disgusted owner of sixty-four fresh ox tongues. A wrong tone of voice had done all the mischief.

The foregoing statements apply accurately to the Chinese language as spoken by at least four fifths of the population. While in certain regions there are slight local peculiarities of pronunciation and idiom, these are nowhere sufficiently serious to deserve mention with a single exception. This exception consists of a strip of country bordering upon the seaboard, and extending from a point north of Shanghai to the extreme southern limit of the empire. It runs back inland in distances varying from fifty to one hundred and fifty miles. Throughout this region, while the written language is the same as in other parts of China, the spoken tongue is broken up into a number of local dialects. Pronunciation of the characters differs so widely in districts that are contiguous that it is commonly said among that Chinese that "people living upon one bank of a river cannot understand a word uttered by their neighbors upon the other." Since Chinese officials are never allowed to hold posts of duty in the provinces where they were born, those on duty in these districts can only communicate with the people whom they govern by the use of interpreters. Chinese who emigrate to the United States, and, in fact, to other foreign parts, all come from within this area. Hence, with few exceptions, none of them speak or understand the correct, standard Chinese.

A chapter upon the language of China would hardly be complete unless it at least mentioned a nondescript tongue that has sprung up within modern times at the points where foreigners are by treaty allowed to reside and pursue their varied callings. Few of these learn the language, and their only medium of communication with the natives in the transaction of business is through the medium of what is known as "pidgin English." "Pidgin" is the net result of the native attempt to pronounce the word "business." Hence the proper name of the jargon would be "business English." With the exception of a few mongrel words gathered no one knows how or whence, it consists of the Chinese idiom literally translated into English; the pronunciation, however, being varied to suit the exigencies of the native powers of speech and understanding. A couple of incidents will show how absurd and utterly undignified this mode of communication is, and will give all necessary explanation of its peculiarities. The reader may be a trifle astonished and perhaps incredulous at the assertion, which, however, is founded in fact, that nine tenths of the enormous business done between foreigners and natives in China is done by means of this grotesque gibberish.

A young man who called upon two young ladies was gravely informed by the Chinese servant who opened the door: "That two piecey girlo no can see. Number one piecey top side makee washee, washee. Number two piecey go outside, makee walkee, walkee." By which he meant to say that the elder of the two was taking a bath upstairs, and the younger had gone out.

When King Kalakua, of the Hawaiian Islands, was in Shanghai in April, 1881, he occupied a suite of rooms up one flight of stairs at the Astor House. Two American gentlemen, desiring to pay their respects to His Majesty, went to the hotel one morning, and meeting the proprietor at the foot of the stairs, made known their errand, and inquired if the king was in. "I will see," replied the landlord, and turning on his heel, he shouted to a Chinese servant at the head of the stairs: "Boy! That piecey king top side hab got?" "Hab got," laconically responded the servant. "Gentlemen," said the landlord, "His Majesty is in. Pray walk up."

CHAPTER IV.

CHINESE HOME LIFE.

In one respect at least China sets an example which all the world may wisely follow. In this empire every one marries, and no one "boards." Hence, generally speaking, there are as many wedded couples as there are men and women above the marriageable age, and as many present and prospective centres of home life as there are couples married. Bachelors and old maids are conspicuous only because of their absence.

Marriage, however, seldom means an immediate, new, and independent home centre. It does not emancipate the man from his duty to his parents, nor lessen in any degree the obedience and support he is bound to render them. He never becomes of age and gains his independence so long as they live. A newly married pair invariably take up their residence with the parents of the groom. In fact, the essential part of the ceremony is the conveyance of the bride in a red sedan chair to the residence of the groom's parents, and the delivery of her to him there. By this act she loses all connection with her own home, her own family, and becomes an integral part of that of her husband.

And in it she does not appear to be primarily the wife of her husband so much as the servant, the drudge, of her mother-in-law.

The lot of the young married woman in China is hard and unenviable in the extreme. She has no voice in the selection of the man to whom she is to be joined, but, theoretically at least, marries one whom she has never seen and to whom she has never spoken. Upon the day appointed for the ceremony she is carried and delivered to him literally like "a cat in a bag," for her head and body to the waist are thus enveloped. He, upon his part, has never seen her, had no share in making the selection, and has not the least reason to be other than wholly indifferent to her. Hence, while mutual affection may come after marriage, it never precedes it, and has no share in the bond which binds the two together. In her new home she simply becomes a convenient under-servant. The most menial tasks, the heaviest burdens are laid upon her. Her only justification for continuing to live is found in child-bearing. Prior to that event she is not ordinarily given the title of a married woman, but is still spoken of or addressed as a girl. In China, not marriage, but motherhood, changes a woman's title from Miss to Mrs. When she becomes a mother, and especially if she bears a son, then at last she is entitled to a certain amount of respect and recognition as something higher than a beast of burden. But before this event occurs young wives not infrequently commit, or attempt, suicide as the only escape from the intolerable cruelties of the mother-in-law.

In motherhood alone does the Chinese woman find protection and honor. Yet even here her position, viewed from a Western standpoint, is peculiar and perhaps grotesque. She may be an auto-

GROUP OF CHILDREN.

crat with her children. She may claim absolute obedience from them, even when they are grayheaded and perhaps themselves fathers of families. She may become, in turn, the terror of several daughters-in-law, and wreak upon them the heavy load of misery she endured as a young wife. But she is never anything but a servant to her husband. In the event of her death her sons must, by Chinese law, wear mourning and go about with unshaven heads for a period of one hundred days. But her husband would render himself an object of ridicule and contempt among his friends if he put on mourning or expressed grief at her loss. He may marry again as often as he sees fit, but it is not considered respectable for a widow to take a second husband. The Chinese, with their usual dislike for plain speech upon any disagreeable subject, never say, "Widow Wang has married again," but "she has taken a step in advance." If a young Chinese widow desires the praise and honor of all her nation, and perhaps a monumental arch erected by command of the Emperor to celebrate her virtues, she will put an end to her own existence upon her husband's coffin. If she is ambitious in a more moderate degree, she will devote the entire remainder of her life to attendance upon the parents of the man whose name she bears.

In conversation with some high officials of the government of China, I once referred to the recent death of the wife of the Prince Regent, and remarked that of course the prince would go into retirement and lay aside his duties for a time.

"Oh, no," replied one of the Cabinet with a laugh; "the death of a wife counts for nothing with us. Why should the prince go into mourning for her? He can get as many more as he wishes."

In point of fact, he already had several others on hand. In China a man is legally and morally allowed to marry as many wives as he can support.

The first, or proper wife, appears to have a certain amount of precedence over the others. They are all servants, among whom she is the head. The children by all are equally legitimate, and have equal rights of inheritance. That this rule is literally carried out is shown by the fact that the Emperor, who seldom marries less than four " head wives," and has anywhere from seventy-five to a hundred " assistant wives," as they are called, or concubines, as we should call them, is supposed to study the characters of all his sons by all these head and assistant wives, and to select from the entire number that one best qualified to succeed him upon his imperial throne. His selection, as might be expected, not infrequently falls upon the son of some favorite concubine, who thus becomes his successor. Chien Lung, one of the ablest rulers of China in many hundred years, was the fourteenth son of his father. And Tung Chih, who died in 1875, and of whom so much cannot be said, was the son of a subordinate wife.

Yet among the middle and poorer classes one wife is practically the universal rule, to which exceptions are very rare. Some of my readers may be inclined to discover a relationship between the fact that, while any number of wives is permissible, more than one is seldom taken, and that other fact, already mentioned, that in the written language of the empire one woman under a roof means " peace," two women under a roof mean " discord," and three, intrigue in its worst form. It would not be at all surprising if some relationship did exist between these widely separated facts.

The Chinese is both practical and of a philosophical turn of mind. It would not be strange if he had seen fit, in this way, to build into the very structure of his language a monument which should for all time give expression of his judgment as to the unwisdom of polygamy.

It should not be inferred, from what has been said, that woman plays no other part in Chinese home life than one of service and drudgery. She has absolute control of her daughters until they are lost to her by marriage into other families. She to a large extent shapes the lives of her sons, and commands their full obedience from their birth until her death. The old women of a Chinese village not only dissect and disseminate all the gossip and scandal afloat in the community, but have a very influential part in determining public opinion. They form what may be called an undertow of influence in village affairs, and often decide matters with which they have no apparent connection. This might be expected from the autocratic position occupied by them in regard to their sons. During more than thirty years two women, the wives of the Emperor Hsien Fêng, and known to foreigners as the Empress Dowager and Empress Mother, have practically controlled the domestic and foreign affairs of China. In all important crises their judgment and will have been accepted as final authority, and have determined the policy of the government. Yet, in obedience to Oriental etiquette, they live in such strict seclusion that, when a council of State becomes necessary, they are indeed present, but concealed by a curtain. Their voices are heard by the members of the Cabinet, but their faces are never seen. One of them died some few years ago, but the other is still vigorous, active, and potential in public affairs.

These two women exactly illustrate the peculiar position occupied by women in the Chinese Empire. As wives they apparently have no influence whatever ; as mothers they are all-powerful. During the life and reign of their husband, Hsien Fêng, the two were merely the puppets of his pleasure. They were unheard, unthought of in any other capacity. But with his death, in 1862, came their period of power which, in the case of one of them, has lasted until the present time. And this is all the more remarkable as showing maternal control to be an actual power, in view of the fact that for nearly twenty years of this period—since January, 1875—the nominal Emperor has not been the son of either of these women. He is a nephew of their deceased husband. Yet his respect and obedience to the will of his aunt are absolute.

Then it is as true in China as everywhere else that a stronger will and character always dominates the weaker. Instances are not rare in which the Chinese wife, hedged in and bound down by the most rigid rules of custom and law, uneducated and unrecognized except as a sort of upper servant, guides and controls her husband, and makes him the mere echo of her opinion. Still further, a Chinese woman never forgets that she has a tongue. Whatever may be her capacity in other directions, in shrill and voluminous scolding she has no equal. Whoever has once listened to a good specimen of her efforts has noticed how the very atmosphere seems to quiver and collapse under the torrent of abusive language which is poured forth, picturesque in its adjectives, and, fortunately, untranslatable into English. Whoever has once heard this will readily believe that in her tongue the Chinese wife possesses a weapon against which man has no defence. He must either run or surrender. He receives no comfort from his masculine neighbors. They jeer at and ridicule him, not at all from sympathy with the wife, but because he has failed to keep her in proper, that is to say *quiet*, subjection.

The ties of locality are very strong among the Chinese, and hence new families, as they are formed, are commonly established in the immediate vicinity of that from which they sprung. In this way one sees groups or nests of families gathered about the parent stock. Whole villages may be found composed almost exclusively of persons of the same name, and containing four or five generations of the same family. "Smithville," "Jonesville," or, to translate more exactly, "The Village of the Chang Family," "The Town of the Wang Family," "The Li Family Cross-Roads"—these and similar names of hamlets, villages, and cities are so frequent throughout China that they form a large fraction of all the names of places in the empire. The property of each family, and more particularly the real estate, is largely held and worked in common, and divisions of it only occur upon the death of the male head of the name. All members of the family, old and young, male

STREET SCENE IN PEKING.

and female, take part in the labor. If it is a farm, all go to the fields together at daybreak and spend the day at work. Women are as commonly seen engaged in such labor as men. I once saw a Chinese farmer holding a plough which was drawn by a cow, a donkey, and his wife, the three harnessed and pulling together.

The class of "globe trotters," as they are somewhat irreverently called—persons of wealth, who travel about the earth sight-seeing—form a never-solved puzzle to the Chinese. His home ties are very strong. He never travels for pleasure, and never leaves home except when obliged to do so upon either public or private business. While absent, whether in foreign lands or in some other part of his own country, he always looks upon himself as an exile, is always more or less homesick, and, no matter how dirty and squalid his native village may be, he looks forward to his return to the wretched place as the chief joy of his life.

The Chinese is not, and cannot become, a colonist without an entire change of his natural disposition. True, he is found in America, North and South, in the Australasian colonies, in Burmah, Siam, the East Indian Archipelago, in Java, and Japan. But in none of these places is his stay permanent. He is nowhere a colonist, but a temporary migrant. He resembles closely the migratory flocks of birds who feed in one region for many months, but build their nests and rear their young invariably in some spot well remembered but far distant. He is driven by emergency away from home, goes into what he considers as exile, but has all his plans for return carefully made before he sets out, and these plans and the hopes connected with them are never absent from his mind. A careful examination of the lists of steerage passengers upon the various lines of steamships running between China and the foreign countries to which the Chinese go, if the examination were so extended as to cover a considerable term of years, would show that practically all who leave the empire return again. They come and go like the migratory birds just mentioned. Those who are so unfortunate as to die in exile have almost invariably made arrangements by which their bodies shall be carried back to their native village, there to rest with their ancestors. It would astonish the people of this land could they know the total number of Chinese who have been in it during the past twenty years, and compare that total with the marvelously small number of graves of the Chinese found among us. And those whose bones have been left to lie permanently here were, beyond question, waifs, poor unfortunates without home ties or friends in their native land.

The Chinese is an acute and careful merchant, a patient, faithful, and diligent laborer, but, above everything else, he is a lover of his home. While he wanders all over the earth, and submits to all sorts of privations, abuses, and hardships, he is only a wanderer whose deepest, all-absorbing desire is for home, a quiet old age with his family, and, more important than all else, burial in the tomb of his fathers. This is true of him not only when necessity drives him into foreign lands, but equally so when he establishes himself in some other part of his own empire. It is not so much a love of China that determines him in this peculiarity as a local tie. A Cantonese never becomes a permanent resident of Peking, for example. He may go there on business—many of them do; but they are always "pilgrims and strangers," and their plans invariably culminate in a permanent home in the village of their birth. If one of them dies in Peking, poor and friendless, the charitably disposed see to it that his body is sent home for burial. There are guilds, or benevolent societies, organized in every large city in the empire, one of the principal objects of such organization being to send home for burial such unfortunates as have died away from their families. The so-called "Six Companies" of San Francisco, about which so much and so many lies have been written, has this among the other purposes of their organization. A traveler in China will occasionally meet a coffin carried suspended between two long poles, and the ends of these poles fastened to the pack-saddles of two mules. Upon the head of the coffin is a wicker crate containing a white rooster. The coffin contains the body of some man who has died away from home, and is being thus carried, perhaps across the entire stretch of the empire, to its proper resting-place. The rooster, which must be of spotless white, unblemished by a single black feather, is supposed to guide or lead the soul of the dead man in the long journey, or to persuade it to accompany the material part. And the livelier the young rooster is, the more he struts about in his cage and crows, the more successful he is supposed to be in the performance of his function.

This intensely strong tie of locality, developed, strengthened, and intensified as it has been through a thousand generations, is reinforced by what is to them a religion, and thus a final return, alive or dead, becomes a sacred necessity in the heart of every Chinese. Reference of course is made to the so-called "worship of ancestors."

While we may and must condemn this worship as a form of idolatry, I must confess that I have never seen a Chinese coffin being carried, either by sea or by land, on its long journey back to the native village of its occupant, without being reminded of the beautiful bit of history found in the early part of the Bible, in which it is written that Abraham bought a field and a cave for a burial-place for Sarah, his wife, in Hebron. Abraham himself was buried there, and so were Isaac and Rebecca. After the death of Jacob, Joseph and his brethren carried the body of their father from Egypt back to Canaan, and laid it there beside Leah. Joseph exacted a promise from his children that his ashes too should be laid in the same tomb. And this promise was fulfilled two centuries after his death. Surely one can hardly fail to respect in the Chinese a feeling which they have in common with the earliest members of the human family, and which they have carried into practice during thousands of years.

The Chinese Government has taken advantage of this peculiarity of the people in a curious way. One of the essential conditions required of any foreigner who may desire to become a naturalized subject of China is that he should own a graveyard, have a burial-place within the limits of the empire. Such ownership is regarded as final evidence of his intention to become a permanent resident.

In another way the government has for many centuries exercised its influence in a manner calculated to keep the people at home, and to minimize and counteract any tendency to change either their residence or occupation. One of the sections of the Code of Laws orders that persons and families truly represent their profession in life, and refrain from altering it. "Generation after generation, they must not change nor alter it"—so the statute reads. The wisdom of such a law in its effect upon a people already too little inclined to favor change of any sort may, perhaps, be questioned. To-day it is practically a dead letter. But it has had a double influence upon the nation. It has caused them to hand down their various callings and occupations from father to son without variation or improvement in methods or processes. It has, at least, had a part in restraining China from all progress, until she is centuries behind the age. And it has, indirectly, segregated the people. A man naturally remains where his business is; and if that business must be that of his father, he naturally follows it where he finds it—at home. His interests centre there, and he seldom wanders far afield.

I once asked an old man whom I saw leaning against the sunny side of a mud wall, as a slight protection from the piercing January wind, how far it was to a Chinese city where I was planning to spend the night. He replied that he did not know. Surprised and incredulous at his answer, I asked him whether he too was a traveler. "Oh, no!" he said; "I live just over there," nodding his head at a comfortable-appearing Chinese house not a hundred yards distant. "How long have you lived there?" asked I. "All my life," said he, "and I am seventy-eight years old." "And you do not know how far it is to such a city?" persisted I, incredulous at his statement. "No. Why should I?" he responded. "I have never been there." This was more amazing still. "You are seventy-eight years old, have lived here all your life, and never been there!" I exclaimed. "Of course not," the old man stoutly retorted. "Why should I go there? I *live here*." The city named was less than ten miles distant!

The effect of the law mentioned in encouraging the permanence of all things, though not in the wisest sense of that word, may have another illustration. In every city of considerable size in China there will be found a certain number of shops for the repair of clocks and watches. No such articles are manufactured in China, few people own them, and the importation is comparatively small. A traveler might be interested to learn where these shops find their customers, and, above all, where they learned their trade. The answer is simple. They know little or nothing of their business. They are invariably Roman Catholics, and inherited both their religion and their calling from their ancestors, who were converts and students of the very early Catholic missionaries in China, more than two hundred years ago. And they only know as much, or as little, of clock and watch repairing as the missionaries were able to teach their ancestors then.

"Honor thy father and thy mother" is a command so inwrought into the very fibre of the Chinese nature, so sustained by public opinion, and so

WALL ABOUT PEKING.

carefully reinforced by law, that he who neglects it even in a small degree, if he escapes punishment as a criminal, is certain to be driven from society as a reprobate and a heathen. It is, in fact, carried to such an unreasonable extreme that it has practically become a form of tyranny. It leaves no room for independent action or personal judgment, and a man cannot exercise his individual powers of manhood until he is too far advanced in years to have their exercise productive of growth or any other beneficial results. At the same time, one of the most pleasing features of Chinese home life is the deference and respect shown to their elders by the younger members of the household. Such nondescript creations as half-grown boys superior in imaginary wisdom and in practical experience with the seamy side of life to their fathers are unknown there. Such phrases as " the old man," " the governor," " the old woman" are not found in the language—at least as applicable to parents. Age is invariably respected and honored. A ragged, dirty, and foul-mouthed beggar-woman upon the streets has so much of reverence shown to her gray hairs that she is never addressed with any other term than " lao tai tai"—" venerable lady." Gray-headed ministers of State, burdened with heavy cares of office, still find time to attend upon their mothers, who may be toothless, blind, and petulant with the fretfulness of second childhood, with the same assiduous care and obedience to all their unreasonable whims that they were taught to give in boyhood. If old age is, indeed, the reward of filial obedience and honor, then the average length of life in China ought to be greater than anywhere else on earth.

Sometimes this respect and affection is shown in what would seem to us as a questionable form, but it is always in accordance with Chinese ideas of propriety. It is no uncommon sight in Peking or any other city of the empire to see a company of men, headed by a band of music and many banners, parading the streets in a long procession, at the centre of which are two coffins. The absence of white, which is the national mourning color, the lively strains of music, and the general air of pleasure throughout the members of the party, makes it certain that they are not performing the last sad rites for the dead. The two coffins have been purchased by the sons of, say, Mr. and Mrs. Chang, as a slight token of filial affection and honor. And they are being carried with great pomp and display to the home of the old people, to whom they will be presented with pleasant speeches and appropriate replies from the surprised recipients. By us such a present would be regarded much as we regard the action of a friend who pulls out his watch in the midst of a call we are making upon him as a hint that we had best be taking our departure. But Chinese parents have no such squeamish notions. They accept these finely lacquered and decorated coffins as a final proof of the forethought and affectionate care of their children. They are placed in the state apartments of their home, carefully protected from injury, and shown with great pride to their friends. The Chinese may not have expensive pianos in their drawing-rooms, but they are frequently provided in advance with the casket which is to furnish their last resting-place; and this, if less noisy, is equally satisfying to their pride. The lugubrious side of the gift never strikes them. They see in it only the love, respect, and forethought of their children. It assures their minds upon one point which is of great importance to a Chinese: it is a present pledge of an honorable, dignified funeral.

It may be said in passing, though not strictly germane to the subject of this chapter, that the Chinese often provide themselves with coffins years in advance of death, and when in robust health. These are carefully put aside against the day of need. A childless widow, for many years in my employ, as a result of the closest economical use of her wages of $4 a month, at last was able to save a sum necessary to buy herself a coffin of plain, uncarved, and unvarnished cedar. Having no home in which to store it, she accepted the offer of a distant relative, a farmer living several miles out of town, to give it room in his house. For three years she made semi-annual pilgrimages upon a donkey to this place of storage in order that she might assure herself that her coffin was safe and kept in good order. But at last she returned from one of these journeys heartbroken, with her tale of woe. Her relative, being hard pressed for money, had pawned her coffin, and then had put the climax upon her disaster by selling the pawn-ticket. Undismayed by this unfortunate experience, the old woman began again to save funds, only a cash or two at a time, with which to buy another coffin; but cholera seized her before the task was completed, and friends gave her the desire of her heart, a decent burial.

CHAPTER V.

CHINESE SOCIAL LIFE.

The Chinese devote little time to amusement and recreation. To the poor, who form an immense majority of the population, life is a never-ending struggle against starvation. They rise at dawn and work until dark, have no Sundays or other rest days. They have but three established holidays in the year. Weddings and funerals form their only excitements, and the only luxuries of which they dream are an ounce or two of meat at very rare intervals with their invariable food of rice and cabbage, and the necessary tea and tobacco. With them half a day of idleness means half a day of hunger, and they appear to lack both opportunity and capacity for what is called social enjoyment. The middle class are extremely busy, but appear to take life more easily. Many of the officials have an excess of leisure, but those who are high in office and in favor with the Emperor are sadly overworked.

I once asked a member of the Chinese Cabinet, who was complaining of fatigue and exhaustion, for a statement of his daily routine of duty. He replied that he left home every morning at two o'clock, as he was on duty at the palace from three until six, and if the Emperor was to give him audience upon public affairs, the interview always took place before dawn. As a member of the Privy Council, he was engaged in that body from six until nine. He was President of the War Department, and hence was there from nine until eleven. Being an officer of the Supreme Court, he was necessarily in daily attendance upon that body from eleven until two. And as he was the senior and responsible minister of the Foreign Office, he spent the hours from two until five or six there every afternoon.

These were his regular daily duties. In addition to them, he was frequently appointed upon special commissions, boards of inquiry, or to posts involving additional labor, and these he sandwiched in between the others as well as he could. He stated that he never reached home before seven or eight o'clock in the evening, and that his connection with his family was merely nominal, as he was never able to eat a meal with them, and really knew less about them than he did about the affairs of his master, the Emperor. Restaurants are connected with all the various offices mentioned by him, and at these, when he had time, he got his food. He died six months after the conversation here reported, literally of overwork and exhaustion.* Other able Chinese officials have been known to sacrifice their lives in the same way. Indeed,

---

* This statement was originally given to the public, several years ago, in an article written for the *Youth's Companion* by the author of this volume.

CARRIAGE OF CHINESE OFFICIAL.

they have no possible way of escape. The will of the Emperor is a final command, and they can only struggle on, overtaxing both brain and body, until one or the other gives way, or the utter collapse of both sends them into a premature grave. Such men take no part in Chinese social life.

Oriental ideas of society are based upon a very different model from those in Western lands. They are so hampered and confined by conventionalities, etiquette, and peculiar notions of what is proper and becoming, that general society, as we use the phrase, thereby meaning the intermingling of the two sexes, is absolutely impossible. There are no social occasions or assemblies in the empire where men and women meet as friends and entertain each other. Such modes of harmless amusement are impossible without an entire reformation of the Chinese social code. The rules of proper intercourse between the sexes, or, to speak more exactly, the rules forbidding any intercourse of any sort whatever, are rigid, inflexible, and admit of no exceptions.

The Chinese, even in the case of old friends, never make inquiry as to the health of the female members of each other's families, or refer to them in any way. With them the question, "How is your wife?" which is so common and innocent a civility elsewhere, would be regarded as discourteous and insulting, even between acquaintances of years' standing. Men who have grown gray together will inquire about and discuss the qualities of each other's sons with the utmost freedom, but they may never mention the female members of the families, even to ask concerning a little girl only eight or nine years of age. The nearest they may approach this forbidden topic is by the use of a phrase generally interpreted as meaning "your family," but which is, in fact, far less direct and to the point than that expression. An illustration of this social law is worthy of being recited.

In May, 1875, news reached Peking that an honored Chinese official, then resident in the United States, had married an American lady. Soon after the receipt of this intelligence, the United States Minister and I had occasion to visit the Chinese Foreign Office. The minister informed me that he intended to congratulate the Chinese officials upon this marriage. I advised him that it was contrary to Chinese notions of propriety to refer to such subjects, and that his remarks would be misunderstood. However, when the party were, as usual, seated around a table at the Foreign Office, tea had been served, and the ordinary salutations exchanged, the minister requested me to say to Prince Kung, then at the head of the government, that "the relations between the United States and China, which had been of so friendly a character for many years, ought to be much strengthened by the fact that a distinguished Chinese officer had married a pretty Yankee girl." I again remonstrated with the minister, but upon his renewed request, I repeated this remark in Chinese to the prince. We were seated around a circular table, and besides the prince and two foreigners there were present six members of the Cabinet, venerable and gray-headed men. For a moment there was a dead silence. Each minister of State looked down at his plate. None dared to speak. Then Prince Kung raised his head, looked at me for another moment in silence, and, drawing a long breath, remarked : " It is fearfully hot to-day." This was the sole outcome of our minister's well-meant but ill-timed congratulations.

Not only are mixed assemblages of the two sexes forbidden by the Chinese social code, but husband and wife are not expected to appear together in public. There are necessary modifications to this rule, as, for example, when families are traveling long distances. Even in such cases the female members of the family have their own servants, who look after their comfort, and the master ignores their presence as far as possible. In point of fact, the entire domestic relationship which every man in China has is universally and absolutely ignored and tabooed. Every one knows, as a matter of course, that it exists, but no one ever mentions or recognizes it. A Chinese gentleman very rarely appears upon the street with his wife, and, when he does, never walks beside, but follows her. And under no circumstances could he be induced to ride in the same carriage with her. It would irretrievably ruin his reputation to do so.

An amusing wrangle which once took place in Peking between a foreigner and a party of Chinese muleteers illustrates Oriental prejudice upon this point. A party of foreigners were setting out in mule litters—large sedan chairs borne by two mules—on a journey of five days. One gentleman desired, for the sake of company, to occupy the same litter with his wife. With a little crowding it could be made to carry two persons. The muleteers at once protested, and refused to proceed. They insisted that it was a gross breach of Chinese propriety, and that they would be abused and jeered at throughout the journey. And they more than hinted that if the foreigner cared nothing for his own or his wife's reputation, they must protect theirs, and they would not be parties to any such scandalous proceedings. No persuasion and no offer of extra wages would move them. To them it was a question of morals, not of money. The scheme was of necessity abandoned.

Another incident somewhat in the same line deserves record, since it shows how very broadly our ideas of social intercourse between persons of opposite sexes differ from the Chinese, and also what serious injury may be done by running counter to their prejudices. The headquarters of the Chinese students who were some years ago sent to this country to be educated, under the care and at the expense of the Chinese Government, were in Hartford, Conn. Some of the young men went to church and Sunday-school. One of them, walking home from church one afternoon American fashion—which is to say, with a young lady—met the Chinese director of this educational mission, as it was called, out driving. The young gentleman politely bowed, and removed his hat to his superior. The conservative old disciple of Confucius could hardly credit his eyes. Here was one of the boys under his charge, for whose moral and mental training he was responsible, actually walking in full daylight upon the streets with a young woman

who was neither his sister nor his first cousin.
This fact alone was quite sufficient to stamp the
reputation of both the young people as hopelessly
bad. But to complete his offence, the young man

FRONT OF OFFICIAL RESIDENCE.

had the effrontery to remove his hat before his
superior, an act which of itself was a grave breach
of Chinese etiquette. The incident was reported
to Peking, where it was looked upon, as the director

himself viewed and characterized it, as an evidence that the students had quite lost their good manners and sense of decency. With other and more serious causes, it led to the recall of the entire body of students, and the abandonment of the enterprise.

Chinese ladies do a considerable amount of calling, and have other social duties, exclusively among themselves. They evidently have the same questions of dress and fashions to discuss that their sisters in other lands find so absorbing. While the cut of their garments never changes, being exactly the same to-day as it was two centuries ago, the style of decoration varies from year to year. They never shop except in the retirement of their own apartments, to which all articles which they may desire to purchase are taken. It is said that they gamble and even take opium "socially," but of the truth or falsity of the statement I have no certain knowledge. It is difficult to conceive what amusement they can have, or how they manage to pass the hours, either in their own homes or when congregated together at social afternoon feminine teas. They do no work, as a retinue of servants is provided to attend to all household duties. None of them can either read or write. As an evidence that they are ladies, and as such above labor of any sort, their finger-nails are allowed to grow to an extraordinary length—to such length, in fact, that they wear gold or silver "nail sheaths," much as a sewing woman wears a thimble—that is to say, it is fitted to the finger in the same manner, and extends the length and in the natural curve of the nail which it encases. Tiny bells dangle from it by delicate chains. This fashion effectually prevents them from busying their fingers with those trifling bits of fancy work with which ladies in other lands occupy so many spare moments.

The women of the poorer classes appear to have absolutely no ideas beyond the range of household drudgery and food and clothing. True, they love to gather, two or three of them, under the shade of a tree in summer, or on the sunny side of a wall in winter, and exchange bits of gossip about neighborhood affairs. But no idea of a social gathering, in the Western sense of the phrase, can be said to have found its way into their minds. A foreign lady once invited several of these poor women, neighbors and acquaintances of each other, to spend the afternoon with her, and provided for them a very simple entertainment of buns and tea. In due time these articles were placed upon the table, and the hostess, being called from the room for a few moments, asked her guests to help themselves. Upon her return she found that they had carefully counted out to each woman her share of the buns, an odd one being divided with the most exact justice between them all, and each had taken her share and a cup of tea to a corner of the room, where she refreshed herself in silence.

In Chinese country life some of these strict rules of separation between the sexes are, in a very moderate degree, set aside. The inhabitants of a village will raise a small sum by subscription, with which to construct a cheap mat-shed for a stage, and employ a company of strolling actors to perform for a day or two at the time of the spring and autumn festivals. All members of the various families attend these; but the women and girls are carefully seated by themselves in a reserved space, and opportunities for general intercourse are very slight. In the larger cities ladies sometimes attend the theatres, which there are permanently established, but they always occupy secluded and carefully screened boxes. It is naturally impossible that in village life, where men and boys, women and children, all go together to the fields at dawn and work there together until dusk—that under such circumstances the same absolute restraints should be enforced as in the easier seclusion of town life. Yet it is astonishing how keenly the sharp eyes of the old women in such a company of laborers watch the younger women and men, and how little of familiar conversation is allowed between them.

There is another reason aside from this separation of the sexes which renders many of what we are accustomed to regard as among the highest pleasures of social life impossible in China. They are totally at variance with Chinese ideas of enjoyment. It is related that the first Chinese minister to this country was once invited to a reception in Washington, where dancing was the principal feature of the evening's entertainment. After watching the flushed and heated dancers for some time in undisguised amazement, and contrasting their violent exercise with their elegant and manifestly expensive costumes, he turned to a friend and inquired: "Why do they do that hard work? Cannot they afford to hire some one to do it for them?"

The accuracy of this story cannot be verified; but if it is not true, it ought to be, as it exactly represents the Oriental idea of much of what we consider as pleasure. His conceptions have been fixed in a totally different mould. He has, indeed, but one model in life—the Confucian. A gentleman must be, above and before everything else, dignified and stately in his motions. To walk rapidly is an offence; to run is absolutely vicious. And to him whirling about on a polished floor would, if men alone were engaged in it, be almost a proof of insanity. But when men and women engaged in it locked arm in arm, if his notions of politeness allowed him to characterize his view of the amusement, it would be in terms far from complimentary. The female sex has no place in his idea of respectable pleasures, nor has violent exercise of any sort a place in his category of gentlemanly amusements.

Chinese gentlemen visit and entertain each other to a considerable extent. But their laborious code of etiquette, elsewhere described, is so cumbersome and vexatious in its details regarding the reciprocal duties of host and guest as to destroy all spontaneity of action, and make entertainment a burden rather than a pleasure. If, in calling upon a friend, one is met at the door by that person, and then he must spend five minutes with him in a polite wrangle over the question which shall first pass the portal, it being absolutely certain at the outset which shall eventually do so; and if this ready-made sort of politeness must be repeated over and over again, when the visitor takes his seat, when he receives the inevitable cup of tea, and at every other point and movement of the interview—if making social calls involves all this, as it does in Chinese polite society, then it is easy to see how closely social intercourse comes to being a bore and a nuisance.

Many Chinese gentlemen have fine libraries of ancient Chinese authors, and are able to talk intelligently and with great interest about their own literature. Many of them, too, make a special study of antique porcelains, jades, coins, lithographs and paintings, all of Chinese origin, and to one somewhat familiar with these subjects they make most charming companions. In discussing questions relating to such subjects the foreigner naturally finds himself in the position of a learner, his Chinese host being his instructor. And he will show such careful research, such patient detail in his investigations, as to astonish his pupil and arouse his admiration.

It requires a peculiar course of instruction, only obtainable by experience, before a man having Western ideas can come into anything approaching familiar social intercourse with a Chinese gentleman. Each has to make so many allowances for the other, their courses and systems of education have been so different, their mental methods are so diverse, their respect for standard authorities rests upon such dissimilar foundations—in short, each finds so many points of what he regards as gross ignorance in the other, that two such men can only come by slow processes, and by a gradually developed mutual forbearance, to be familiar friends. By way of illustration, we should hardly expect to find a man able to reason closely and logically on points of mental and moral philosophy who did not know that the earth was spherical, and who could not possibly be made to understand that a traveler wishing to go from New York to Peking would be equally certain of reaching his destination either by traveling east or west. Yet there are many such men in the Chinese Empire. One would not expect to find an acute and sagacious statesman in a person who had never heard of the law of gravitation, and who was confident that an eclipse was caused by a dog in the heavens endeavoring to devour either the sun or the moon, as the case might be. Yet there are such. It seems strange to us that a person could be a master of style in composition, and have a wide and well-deserved reputation as an elegant and polished writer, yet be ignorant of the simplest fundamental elements of what to us constitutes an education. Yet there are many such examples.

The Chinese gentleman—he is always a literary graduate—is fond of an argument. He has his own system of logic, and reaches his conclusions on what may seem at times to us to be whimsical and even absurd grounds. He is acute, quick to detect flaws in the chain of reasoning of his adversary, and to take advantage of them. He always bows to any quotation from the writings of Confucius. He sometimes, to his own satisfaction at least, turns the tables upon his opponent, and makes his own interpretation of certain mutually accepted facts settle in his favor some hotly contested principle. It is from this peculiarity that argument with him has a special interest. It shows how his mind works, and to what extent credulity is made to take the place of broad and well-established general principles.

I once had an argument lasting several hours with a distinguished Chinese scholar who held a high post under the government, over the general proposition, advanced by him, that a fox had the power to turn himself at will into a man. Grotesque as this proposition may appear, we fought over it for the time mentioned, neither apparently making headway against the other, when suddenly my friend and opponent said: "But how can you deny what you know has occurred, as an actual fact, here in Peking? And you yourself are familiar with all the circumstances of the case. A soldier in the British Legation was preparing for bed one night a couple of years ago, when he heard the cry of a fox in the legation grounds. He dressed again, took his rifle, and telling his wife that he was going to kill that fox, went out. Shortly after she heard the report of his rifle, and fell asleep. When she awoke in the morning she was surprised not to find him in the room. A few moments later two of his comrades brought his dead body into the house. He had been found in a clump of laurel bushes, shot through the head. His rifle lay beside him, but the fox was nowhere to be seen. Now, what can be plainer," exclaimed my antagonist most triumphantly, "than the facts of this case? The soldier was chasing that fox through those laurel bushes. He was gaining on him; the fox saw that he was likely to be caught, and so, in the flash of an eye, he changed himself into a man, snatched his rifle from the poor soldier, and shot him through the head with his own weapon. Then he changed himself into a fox again and ran away. Why do you need argument in the face of such facts?" And he, smiling and confident, paused for my reply. My only reply was, and the only possible answer, that I admitted his facts, which indeed were familiar to every person in Peking; but I denied his inferences. The transformation of the fox into human form and his subsequent action were not facts, but inferences. My inferences were that the soldier was crawling upon his hands and knees through the laurel thicket in a stealthy approach to the fox, and that he was carelessly dragging his rifle behind him, having hold of it near the muzzle. A twig caught the trigger and exploded the piece, the charge entering his brain. Thus the argument ended, neither side having won the other to his view. Grotesque as his ideas upon this point of natural history may appear, this Chinese was a wise, sagacious, and broadminded public officer.

Chinese reception-rooms and libraries are fitted up with great elegance, though not, perhaps, in accordance with our ideas of comfort. To recur again to the strict seclusion required of the female portion of any household, it should be noticed that a caller, in approaching these rooms, is expected to make his approach known by a cough, in order to afford them time to retire before he enters. The Chinese are very proud of their sons, and they are allowed to be present, and are exhibited with an assumption of indifference and many formal words of disappointment and regret at their stupidity, all of which is only a barely perceptible veil covering their fondness and pride. The surest way by which to gain a much-desired point with a Chinese father is to see him, if possible, in his own home, and there to admire and praise his sons.

It need hardly be said that all social intercourse between natives and foreigners in China is strictly confined to persons of the same sex. This is unfortunate, no matter from what point it is viewed. But no change is likely until Oriental views of propriety shall be so far relaxed as to conform in some degree to the practice in Western lands. And this is a change which cannot be hastened, and any effort to force it would have an effect in exactly the opposite direction. At present the international gatherings, as they may be called, for social purposes, lacking that which the grace, wit, and beauty of woman alone can give, are, on the whole, dreary festivals. It requires much patience and a philosophic turn of mind to endure them; or perhaps it is better to say that it would require these qualities were there not invariably so large an element of comicality present to enliven the feast.

In dinner-giving in China between Chinese and foreigners, the guests are invariably at the mercy of their hosts. The peculiarities of table service are each so utterly unlike the other, the dishes served are so strange, and the whole code of table manners is so widely diverse, that a dinner of this sort, otherwise tedious, becomes entertaining by reason of the very blunders of the guests, who may

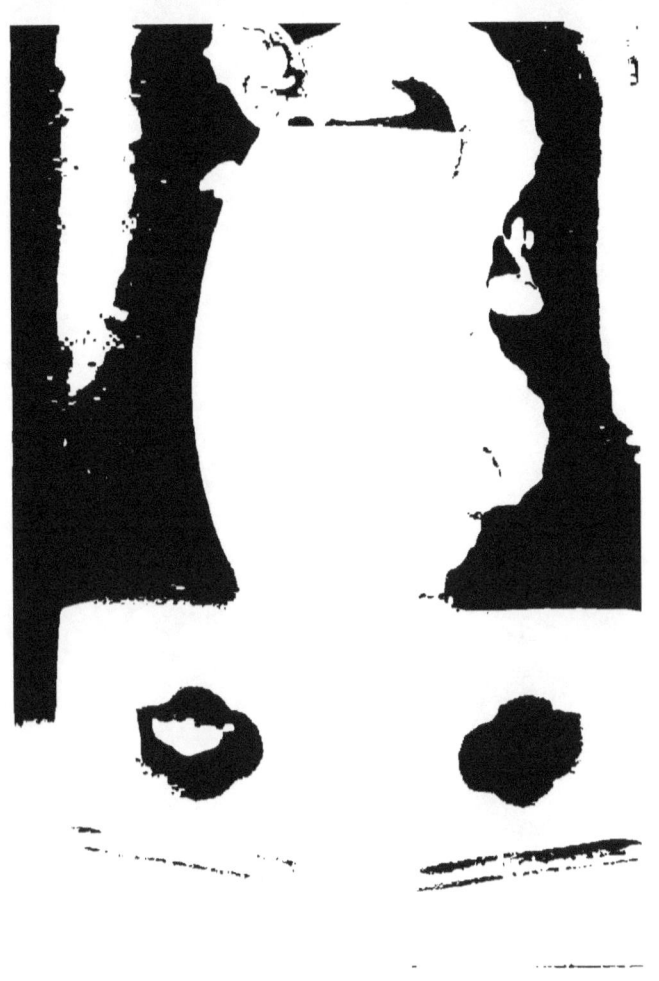

CHINESE DRAGON (MOULDED IN PORCELAIN).

be past-masters in the art of elegant dining upon their own ground, but become blundering schoolboys with strange food strangely cooked and to be eaten with strange utensils. If an American chases a grain of rice all around the circumference of his plate with a pair of chop-sticks when he is a guest at a Chinese dinner, he has his revenge when, at his own table, he watches his former host, after numerous struggles with a knife and fork, gravely abandon them and make free use of nature's utensils—his fingers.

In entertaining strangers from strange lands, one is often amused and also instructed. It was once my fortune to show civilities to a distinguished Corean, a member of the Cabinet, who came to Peking at the head of the annual embassy to the Emperor of China. He was a man of dignified and refined manners; his face showed acuteness and ability, and he was greatly esteemed for his high scholarship and literary ability. Yet the photographic camera and the photographs of himself taken that winter were the first articles of the sort he had ever seen. A kerosene lamp was an utter novelty to him, and he evidently disbelieved the statement that the oil burned in it flowed from the ground. He had never seen, much less set foot within, a foreign residence, and all its varied arrangements and conveniences were of the utmost interest to him. He was startled out of his usual dignified bearing when he seated himself in an upholstered spring-bottomed chair. At a dinner which I gave to him and his colleague, it was almost pathetic to notice how carefully the two Corean gentlemen watched the actions of others at the table, and followed the example they thus found in the use of table implements, and the mode of eating food with which they were wholly unfamiliar. But in the course of the dinner they gave their host an illustration of Corean table manners which was amusing at the outset, and by its ultimate consequences quite upset his gravity. Each Corean brought his body-servant to the dinner, and each servant placed himself behind his master's chair. As they took no part in the service of the table, their presence at first appeared to be purely ornamental, or a sort of necessary exponent of the rank and dignity of their masters. It soon became evident, however, that there were certain emoluments attached to their position; for when the master of either had eaten as much of any course as he cared for, he would pass what remained on his plate, or so much as he could gather in his fingers, over his shoulder to his servant, who would eat it. Thus when, for example, chicken cutlets were served, the master would pass the bone, with some remnants of flesh upon it, to his man, who would gnaw it clean, and gravely drop the bone upon the carpet.

This was amusing, though not specially beneficial to my carpet. However, my revenge came later, when, in an unlucky moment, His Excellency Chin Hong Chi handed to his servant the butt of a particularly large stem of French asparagus. The master had dealt with it as he had seen other gentlemen deal with theirs, and the result was favorable. The servant was not so fortunate. His heroic efforts to chew and swallow the strange article of food made him black in the face, quite upset the gravity of the host, and made him guilty of a grave breach of Oriental etiquette. And the wretched valet probably left the feast disgusted at the bad taste of foreigners, who would serve boiled corn-stalks with melted butter upon their tables, and amazed at the strength of foreign jaws and the sharpness of foreign teeth, which could cope with a vegetable so hopelessly tough.

CHAPTER VI.

CHINESE RELIGIONS.

It is difficult to understand how Confucius has come to be regarded as the founder of a system of religious belief. He is so regarded among many foreigners, and even by some writers who should be better informed. He wrote little or nothing upon what may be termed religious topics further than to endorse and commend certain rites which had been practiced commonly among the people for centuries before he was born. He exhorted his followers to the orderly observance of these rites, but went no further. Though he believed himself commissioned to restore the doctrines and usages of the ancient kings—and he claimed no higher mission than this—he professed to know little or nothing about the higher powers, and never taught that man had a duty to a power higher than the head of his family or of the State. When he was once questioned about divinities, he said that he did not understand much about the gods, and believed that the duty of man lay rather in fulfilling his obligations to his relatives and society, than in the worship of unknown spirits. On another occasion, being questioned regarding sacrifice to spirits, he said : "Not knowing life, how can we know death ?"

Confucius was a moral philosopher, not a religious leader. He was a sage, not a devotee. He elaborated a system of ethics which has stood the test of the centuries, and has had much to do with the conservation of the Chinese nation. But it may well be doubted whether he felt any serious personal interest in the religious observances which he countenanced. If so, his interest lay rather in their antiquity than in any faith in their efficacy. The whole burden of his teachings was in behalf of moderation, order, and what may be termed the lower grades of virtue. He never got beyond the negative form of the golden rule ; and it is extremely probable that he intended not so much to advise the practice of any religious rites as that, if practiced, it should be in a decorous and dignified manner.

Two and a half centuries had passed after his death before the Chinese came to recognize his wisdom in any practical way. Confucius was born B.C. 551, and died B.C. 479. Yet, so far as the historical records show, Kao Tsu, the first emperor of the Han dynasty, was the first to show special reverence and regard for the sage by offering sacrifice at his tomb, about B.C. 200. And it was not until the first year of the Christian era that a temple was erected to his memory by imperial command. Such places of worship and sacrifice must now be numbered by thousands. His memory is venerated by every Chinese, and his word is law throughout the empire. It is astonishing how glibly he is quoted by prince and pauper, whether in the discussion of some grave international question or as an incentive to almsgiving. His word settles street wrangles and determines the policy of the State. He is sometimes quoted under circumstances that render any reference to him grotesque and amusing, and the phrase quoted may not have the faintest apparent bearing upon the question at issue, but it has weight. He is the great arbitrator, authority, and peacemaker of the empire.

The system of so-called religion to which his name has been given was evolved by his disciples and successors from a few obscure phrases in his writings. It is pure materialism, making all things to have originated from the "first element," the primary microbe. This, operating upon itself, produced the dual powers of nature, the male and female elements, and from these, by a process of evolution, all existent forms have sprung. With reference to any creative agency, any God, or any divinities or spirits, one of his most celebrated commentators said: "Sufficient knowledge was not possessed to say positively that they existed, and he saw no difficulty in omitting the subject altogether." He has nothing to say concerning the immortality of the soul or future rewards and punishments. There is little to interest an intelligent student of religious systems in these elaborations of the supposed Confucian idea, or to reward him for his labor. They are, in the main, confused and meaningless repetitions of words whose thought is either uncertain or absent. And it must be borne in mind that they do not represent what he said—for he said little or nothing—but the more or less fanciful conjectures of his followers, some of whom lived many hundreds of years after him, as to what he probably believed.

What is known as the religion of Confucius among foreigners is called, by Chinese, by a term which may be translated as meaning the doctrine of philosophers. The idea is essentially that conveyed by the name " Illuminati," applied to classes of persons at different times in Europe. The rites prescribed by it are the worship of heaven and earth and the worship of ancestors. Essential, though less important, is the worship of the sun and moon. To these has been added, in comparatively modern times, the worship of Confucius. The practice of the last-named rite is confined to officials, actual or expectant, literary graduates, and students. All members of these classes are required to do homage at his shrine. The worship of heaven and earth is practiced by all classes and both sexes. It is an essential part of the wedding ceremonies and other equally important events.

The most elaborate and interesting of all religious structures in China is the Temple of Heaven, at Peking. It has two high altars, one covered and the other open. The most gorgeous and impressive ceremonial in the empire is that which takes place when the Emperor, as son and sole high-priest of Heaven, goes there twice each year to worship. In this service he has neither assistant nor substitute. He prepares himself for this solemn duty by a period of retirement and fasting in a hall within the enclosure specially devoted to that purpose. Without going into the details of the rite, it may be said, in passing, that it bears a most striking resemblance, both in its general features and detail, to the Mosaic ritual as found in the Bible. One feature, however, is peculiar. Ranged in a circle about each altar are large iron crates, shaped like enormous baskets. In these are deposited, at the time of the winter sacrifice, slips of paper, each bearing the name, crime, and other details of some Chinese offender whose life has been taken during the preceding year for offense against the laws. In this way the Emperor makes report to Heaven of the administration of affairs, so far as it has involved the death penalty.

One peculiar feature of the worship at this imperial structure is worthy of notice. Though men and women alike throughout the empire worship heaven and earth, no place is allowed to females in the grand pageant and solemn ceremonial referred to above. Not only are they excluded from all participation in it, but their presence on any part of the grounds at any time is held to be a pollution of the sanctuary. If one of the native guards of the temple should even carry a female infant in his arms into the beautiful park which surrounds and forms the outer enclosure to it, he would be most severely punished.

When General Grant, in the spring of 1879, visited Peking, this temple, for the first time in its history, was officially thrown open. To a Chinese mind it was one of the highest honors that could be paid to him. Some foreign ladies, having learned in advance that the gates were thus to be opened for this distinguished American, took advantage of the fact and made their way into the enclosure, rightly conjecturing that the timid and ignorant guards would imagine that they belonged to the General's party, and hence would not dare to bar the way. As this courtesy had been extended to my guests through me, I felt bound to take an early opportunity to explain the facts to Prince Kung, and to express my regret at the intrusion. He replied at once : " I know all about it. But don't mention the subject, even in a whisper. If it came to be generally known, there would be serious trouble."

The respect, amounting to reverence, which the Chinese feel for education and literature, shows itself in a peculiar adjunct to the worship of Confucius. In every city and large town in the empire the graduates of the literary examinations are organized in a guild or association. They place boxes at street corners, in shops, and other frequented places, upon which is painted the advice : " Have respect for the written character." In these boxes all persons are requested to carefully deposit any scraps or pieces of waste paper which contain printed or written matter. They also sometimes employ men, provided with a basket and a bamboo rod with a sharp nail at the end, to patrol the streets and gather up any such paper that may have been dropped. The contents of these various receptacles are gathered together, and at stated intervals the members of the guild march with them in solemn procession, preceded by a band of music, to the Temple of Confucius. An essential feature of the courtyard of the temple is a small shrine or oven, an illustration of that in Peking

OVEN FOR BURNING PAPER, IN CONFUCIAN TEMPLE, PEKING.

being given herewith. The papers are deposited in this shrine and burned, while these devotees of literature prostrate themselves in worship. Perhaps no one thing gives the educated Chinese such a low opinion of foreign culture and refinement as the careless, indifferent, and, in their eyes, disrespectful way in which we treat printed or written paper. They cannot understand how any person of genuine education would show such lack of regard for the source of all his learning.

The worship of ancestors is literally universal in China. There are no exceptions to the practice except in case of Christianized Chinese, and on no other ground do these receive so much criticism and abuse, amounting in individual cases to persecution, as for their neglect of this solemn duty. So far as can be discovered, the worship is as old as the race. It is the most deeply rooted of all forms of religion in the very fibre of the Chinese character, and, beyond a question, it will be the last of all forms of false faith to die out from among them.

Whatever may be the theoretical idea in the worship of ancestors—and there has been much dispute upon the question—the practical belief under which it holds the hundred of millions of Chinese to observance of the rite is substantially as follows : The masses believe that the spirits of the departed remain near the home occupied by them during life, and the grave in which the body rests. They believe that these spirits are powerful to work good or ill to their descendants, and that hence they must be propitiated by offerings. The more ignorant classes, at least, believe that they are actually supported, fed by the sacrifices placed before their tombs, and that the sham money burned in the ceremony is by some unexplained process transmuted into coin current in the world of spirits, and there serves to pay their expenses. Gross ideas these, beyond a doubt; but they exist and form an animating motive of the worship of ancestors as practiced by a large portion of the people of China. There may be, probably is, an element of filial devotion in the service. But there is also a large element of fear, an anxiety to stand well with the gods, and to secure for themselves the favoring influences which their departed relatives are believed to possess.

This worship makes clear one point of Chinese belief which otherwise might be in doubt. It shows conclusively that they believe in the continued existence of the soul after death. And it makes plain the logic of their conduct in certain other matters, showing that the course so uniformly taken by them is more of a necessity than any mere choice. It explains why there are no bachelors in China. Every man must marry and rear sons to perform this rite, essential to his eternal happiness, at his grave. He must have sons, not daughters, for a double reason. While all members of a given family participate in the ceremonies, the active part of the service must be rendered by sons. And, further, a daughter, when married, ceases to concern herself in the affairs of her own parents, but is absorbed in the family of her husband. This service explains why the Chinese go and come between foreign lands and China, or remote parts of their own country, but practically never colonize, and why such intense stress is laid upon the return of a dead body from no matter how great a distance for burial in the ancestral ground. It is there that this ceremony is observed, and there the body must be to receive the benefit of it. If buried elsewhere, the soul of the departed is doomed to wander in cold, hunger, and desolation.

The ancestral tablet, as it is called, is found in every Chinese home, and, theoretically at least, obeisance before it is made daily. This tablet is a strip of wood set into a wooden base, painted generally red, and having an inscription in gilt upon it to show its purpose. It is generally enclosed in a small shrine more or less carved and ornamented. But the formal sacrifice occurs semi-annually at the tombs. It is elaborate and expensive according to the means of the celebrants. The grave mounds are carefully cleared of grass and weeds, and rounded into shape. A table is spread before the entrance to the place of burial, and upon it the offerings are placed. These ordinarily consist of baked meats of different kinds, pigs and ducks being most common, rice, cakes, wine, and strips of silk, with which the spirits are supposed to clothe themselves. Firecrackers, those universal attendants of all Chinese forms of ceremony, are discharged in large quantities, and large sums of imitation money are burned, thus being transmitted and transmuted for spiritual use by fire.

The Chinese are nothing if not economical. This liberal display of food and drink is *presented* to ancestors, but, after they have gained whatever sustenance may be available in it for them, it is *eaten* and *drank*, down to the last crumb and drop, by the surviving members of the family. Thus the day is made a holiday in the true sense of the word. Instances have been known in which families too poor or too economical to purchase the materials for such a feast have hired them for the day, to be returned in good order at night. Others buy imitation roast pigs and ducks made of coarse pasteboard and painted. They appear to believe that disembodied spirits are more easily imposed upon than are the living.

In order to secure an intelligent conception of the place which the three great religions of China occupy in the minds of the people, it is best to accept the fact that the entire mass of the population —always excepting Christian converts—are believers in Confucianism. That is to say, giving that name to a system of religious practice which he did not originate, and of which he really had very little to say, and understanding its essential features to consist of the worship of heaven and earth and of ancestors, with the worship of the sage himself added later for scholars only, then every true Chinese is a Confucianist. That is the one original, universal, indigenous religion of China. The other two, yet to be described, are, so to speak, supplementary and subordinate. It will do much to free the mind of the reader from confusion if this fact is kept in view.

There has been much discussion whether Taoism was a native or an imported religion, with the balance of opinion inclining toward the latter. Its founder was a Chinese who traveled in other parts of Asia, and all his teachings bear the ear-marks of

Brahminism. He was contemporaneous with Confucius, though a few years his senior, and met him at least once. The name Taoism, or the ism of Tao, gives more than a hint as to the nature of that belief. Tao is a Chinese word, whose first meaning is " road" or " way," and the professed object of the founder of the system was to explain the relations existing between the universe of mind and matter and this Tao. A sentence or two from his writings will show, amusingly perhaps, how easily he set about his task. And they will also most likely give the reader all that he cares to know in detail of this form of belief. Here they are : " All material visible forms are only emanations of Tao or reason ; this formed all beings." Again : " Reason has produced one, one produced two, two produced three, and three made all things. All beings repose on the feminine principle, and they embrace, envelop the male principle ; a fecundating breath keeps up their harmony." His theories remind the student of nothing so much as of a dog chasing its tail. And they are nearly as devoid of sense.

Theoretically Taoism, at least in its original form, did not favor idolatry—that is, the worship of visible objects ; but now it has all imaginable forms of idols, and may almost be said to make new ones to order. Originally it taught asceticism, or at least that the study of pure reason and the mortification of bodily desires formed the sole duty of man. But all this has long since been changed. Taoist priests are the jugglers, astrologers, fortune-tellers, and general mountebanks of

China. The fountain of eternal youth, the elixir of life, and the plant of immortality which grows in some fabulous Eastern isles—these are the stock phrases upon their lips, and ideas springing out of them form the burden of their teaching. They have also adopted (if they did not originate) that old European humbug, and profess to be able to transmute base metals into gold.

It is, to say the least, significant that the official establishment of Confucius as an object of national worship, the birth of Christ, and the introduction of Buddhism into the Chinese Empire should have occurred at about the same time. There is a legend among the Chinese to the effect that, about the time of the birth of the Saviour, the reigning emperor was several times warned in a dream that a wise man would shortly be born in the West, and he was advised to send an embassy to invite him to China. Another legend recites that the emperor dispatched an embassy because of a remarkable expression of Confucius five hundred years earlier, to the effect that " the people of the West have a sage." This much is certain : an embassy was sent to the West about the time of the birth of Christ to seek for a new faith. It wandered into India, and the result was the introduction of Buddhism into the empire.

Buddhist temples are a feature of every landscape in China. They are to be found by scores in the larger cities, by tens in the smaller, and by twos and threes in every market town and village, while no hamlet is so insignificant as to be without its mud god, not unfrequently in a most shocking condition of disrepair. In general, they are built, repaired, and maintained by private subscription, in which public sentiment forces each member of the community to bear his share. Some, however, are supported by annual grants from the government, or by endowment. Those receiving aid from the State are distinguishable by yellow-tiled roofs—yellow being the imperial color, forbidden to the people.

In addition to what may be called formal temples for the worship of Buddha, there are an innumerable number of wayside shrines to be met with all over the country, devoted either to the worship of that deity in person or to some subordinate inferior god in the Buddhist pantheon. Once, when traveling in the province of Shansi, and about half-a-dozen miles distant from a sacred Buddhist spot called Wu Tai Shan, I came across such a wretched little shrine, built of mud, about the size of a dog-kennel, which was dedicated to " The one thousand two hundred and forty-nine unnamed local divinities of the earth, air, and sea." Here was a veritable *omnium gatherum* of a shrine. The big gods have each his own place of worship; but it had occurred to some devout-minded Chinese that there might be a considerable number of little deities left unnoticed yet deserving of attention. He had numbered them all, and consecrated this mud shrine to their service. It was thoughtful, but grotesque.

While the first and fifteenth of the moon and certain feast days are more particularly days of worship, the temples are always open, day and night, throughout the year; a priest is always in attendance to conduct the worship, and a wick floating in a cup of oil furnishes a faint but perpetual light before the images. The worship is always individual, there being no such thing as joint or congregational service known. The ordinary form is very simple, and occupies but a moment. A worshiper comes in, buys for a few cash several sticks of incense from the priest, who lights them for him at the sacred flame. These are handed to the worshiper, who places them in a bronze incense-burner upon a table in front of the image of Buddha. He then prostrates himself upon a rug before the idol three times, each time knocking his head three times upon the floor, the priest meanwhile beating a huge drum or bell to attract the attention of Buddha. This done, the worshiper rises and goes about his business. This is the usual form of worship in all Chinese temples. It is simple, inexpensive, and interferes with neither business nor pleasure. In larger temples, to which a number of priests and neophytes are attached, they are required to be "on watch," much like sailors on shipboard, and at regular periods, night and day, perform this ceremony. The priests are, as a class, notorious for their ignorance and vicious habits. They are not allowed to marry, and probably not one tenth of them can read or write. They learn the exceedingly limited vocabulary of the ritual, which consists of barely more than one or two Sanscrit words, by having it repeated to them.

There is a regularly graded Buddhist hierarchy, culminating with one who may be termed, for lack

of a better name, an archbishop. He is supposed
to be subordinate only to the Grand Llama in
Thibet in ecclesiastical affairs. I exchanged calls
with such an archbishop at Wu Tai Shan, a sacred
resort already mentioned. He was a very pleasant-
faced, mild-mannered old gentleman, aged about
seventy, not a Chinese, but a Thibetan. In consequence he spoke poor Chinese, but we managed to
get on very well in our conversation. He set out
some very choice tea to drink, to which he added
cream (which Chinese never use) and salt. It was
not at all unpalatable. The old man was something of a gossip, manifested the utmost curiosity
and the densest ignorance about all foreign matters, and in the course of a long conversation became very frank and confidential. He informed
me that archbishops were chosen by ballot by the
bishops, from among their own number, for a term
of six years. He had been elected three terms, and
a new election would occur in a few months. He
added naïvely that he doubted whether he would
seek another term. He was rather tired of the
monotony of the post, was getting on in years,
and besides *it cost too much to secure the election.*
The honor, pay, and perquisites were not worth it.

In addition to the regular hierarchy of the priest-
hood, there is an anomalous and comparatively
modern creation known as a "living Buddha."
He is supposed to be an incarnation of the original
Buddha, has no part in the councils of the organization, is of course sacred, and his most unfortunate lot in life is to sit upon a lotus-leaf throne and
be worshiped. Theoretically he never dies, but

goes away, and then is sought for and always found reincarnated in some young boy. With a certain amount of inconsistency, while there was but one original Buddha, there are four modern incarnations of him: one at Lhassa and three at three different and rival sacred centres of the faith in China.

Buddhism has manifestly taken on certain additional ideas, with their corresponding phrases and terms, by being brought into contact and contrast with Christianity. Certain of the most important expressions in Buddhism as taught to-day are not to be found in the original theories of existence and of rewards and punishment. Early Buddhism says nothing about heaven or hell, a personal devil, or a goddess of mercy. Such a figure as that reproduced, and which represents a Buddhist priest treading Satan under his feet, would not have been understood by primitive Buddhists, nor would Quan Yin, the Buddhist Madonna, of whom an illustration is also furnished.

It strikes a Western man oddly, as he passes along the streets of a Chinese city, to see upon the walls, which are as thickly plastered with advertisements of all sorts as those of any city in this land, unless, indeed, the Chinese warning, "Post no Bills," has been put up—it strikes him oddly to read, among flaming notices of quack remedies, the words, "Ask and ye shall receive," or, "To him who asks in faith shall be given." At first he imagines that the American crank has a Chinese brother who is imitating him in placarding texts of Scripture in unseemly places. Such, however, is not the fact. These are simply headlines to ad-

BUDDHIST PRIEST TRAMPLING SATAN UNDER FOOT.

vertisements of Buddhist temples, posted with the desire to secure the prayers, *and hence the cash*—for no pay, no pray, is the rule—of worshipers. They are posted as a matter of business.

The number of mendicant or tramp priests in China must be enormous. They are encouraged and fostered ; by a rule of the order, any priest is entitled to receive, free of cost, a night's lodging and a meal at any temple to which he may apply. The majority of them are professional beggars, and, in order to increase the force of their appeal, which is ordinarily for some imaginary temple at a great distance, adopt artificial deformities, or make special effort to intensify their naturally repulsive appearance. To one such whom I met on the street I offered what was a considerable sum of money to him for the finger-nails of his left hand. He assured me that they had not been cut in ten years, and, judging from appearance, they had not been cleaned in even a longer period. They were fully eight inches in length, curved like a bird's claws, and the thumb-nail stretched like a long arch over and beyond the others, until it ended outside the back of his hand. He was obliged to carry his hand palm uppermost and slightly closed in front of his breast. Those nails would have made a unique curiosity, but the offer made was indignantly declined. With his hair, which, contrary to priestly rule, grew long, under a vow, as he declared, and which, he said, had not been dressed in a decade, which also seemed probable, those nails formed a valuable stock-in-trade.

There is another class of priests who may be

called "professional money-getters." They are attached to no temple, but their services are engaged when extensive repairs or other special emergencies calling for money in unusual sums arise. I saw one of this class in Peking, through whose cheeks circular holes had been cut, and the upper and lower teeth opposite these openings knocked out. Through the path thus made was thrust an iron rod as large as a middle finger, projecting an inch beyond either cheek. A half circle hoop of iron was loosely fastened to either end of the rod and passed around the back of his head. Fastened to this was an iron chain, such as is called a log chain, of sufficient length to drag on the ground for several feet behind him as he passed along the street. He also wore the beggar's robe of a hundred patches, a priestly garment made from small bits of cloth of the utmost possible variety and contrast of color. He was engaged to go from house to house soliciting contributions for the repair of a well-known temple. He was a brazen, bold-faced scoundrel, for whom there was not even a faint call for sympathy. The rod, chain, and ragged garment were his artistically prepared stock-in-trade. He could even simulate bleeding at those circular holes in his cheeks. He received from the temple priests who employed him regular monthly wages, and a fixed percentage of all sums collected.

Another peculiar mode of raising funds for temple repairs deserves notice. A small, box-like structure, only large enough to contain a person standing, is placed in front of the temple. A

GODDESS OF MERCY

priest—and there is a class with whom this form of begging is a specialty—is placed in the box, which is securely fastened. Then sharp-pointed spikes are driven through every available inch of space in the surface of the box—driven in until they come into close contact with every part of the priest's body, and he cannot move an inch in any direction. Only his right hand and forearm are left free, in order that he may, by means of a cord, strike the temple bell, and thus call the attention of passers to his sad condition. A price is then put upon each spike, the sum total, of course, being the amount of money which is needed. The value of each spike is fixed according to its position opposite the priest's body, those opposite the eyes and vital parts being most expensive. The theory of this comedy is that passers-by, seeing the pitiable plight of the holy priest, will be anxious to aid in releasing him. This they can do by buying the spikes which compass him so closely. A priest stands in attendance to extract the spikes as they are paid for and deliver them to the buyers, who have thus lasting souvenirs of their benevolence. Theoretically the imprisoned priest stands in his kennel without relief or interruption, day and night, until every spike has been withdrawn.

Space will allow of only a single incident in illustration of the self-inflicted cruelties and hardships which Buddhism demands of its votaries. One intolerably hot and dusty afternoon I was resting at a wayside tea-house to the southwest of Peking, when I saw a man and a woman approaching and stirring the deep dust of the highway in a very peculiar manner. The man would take one long step forward from a certain point, measure his length, face downward, in the road, then place his feet at the spot marked in the dust by his forehead, take another step, measure his length again, and so proceed, one step and one prostration, as the Chinese call it. At each prostration he knocked his head three times in the dust. The procedure reminded me of the measuring worm of childhood. In answer to my questions, he said that a year before, when his only son was very ill, he had made a vow that, if Buddha would restore the young man to health, he would make a pilgrimage to Wu Tai Shan and back to his native village, making the entire journey in the manner above described. The distance was nearly two thousand miles, and he could measure about three miles a day. As he was seventy-eight years old, frail in appearance, and about worn out, it was easy to see that he would not live to fulfill his vow. A callous lump as large as an egg had formed upon his forehead. Yet this man was shocked and angry at a suggestion that he should abandon his useless pilgrimage, and passed out of sight measuring the road with his feeble body.

The male Chinese is much like his Western brother: he is less religiously inclined in times of prosperity than in seasons of adversity. When the storm arises, then he runs to shelter. Hence, ordinarily women and children form the large majority of the devout at Buddhist shrines. Even they adopt it as a supplementary sort of belief, and habitually disregard some of its most vital tenets.

Thus, for example, eating animal food or taking life in any form is strictly forbidden to all Buddhists. One of the tests of devout Buddhism among the common people is shaped into the familiar, if somewhat disagreeable expression that a true Buddhist will not destroy the vermin found on his own body. Yet one would travel more than one day's journey in China to find a Buddhist who would refuse to eat meat when offered to him. The Chinese common people refrain from animal food not from principle, but from poverty. The same is true regarding the prohibition of winedrinking. And if we turn to the commandment against lying as a test, there is not a good Buddhist in all China.

At the same time, when trouble comes, it is astonishing how this form of belief appears to reassert a secret hold upon the Chinese mind. Men of really great intellectual grasp, of clear and commanding intellect, degrade themselves to the most puerile and ridiculous performances, and spend large sums upon the priests in order to gain some material advantage, or to change a tide of ill-fortune into good. For example, a distinguished Chinese statesman, whose name and presence are known in Europe, and who for this reason shall be nameless here, having been most unjustly degraded from office, and having in vain pulled every wire of family or political influence to secure reinstatement, finally devoted an entire year and a good part of a large fortune to a tour of worship at each one of the numberless temples and shrines in and near

Peking, approaching and leaving each by the "one step and one prostration" just described.

The Chinese as a nation have too much intellectuality and practical good sense to accept very seriously the mass of absurd fanfaronade which constitutes modern Taoism. But unfortunately Buddhism appeals more directly and in a less absurd degree to the weaker side of the Oriental—his superstitious side. And it is because of this that it is so popular and so injurious. That it is an awful force, active in the debasement and deterioration of the national character, no sane man, who has seen it and lived in the midst of it, can doubt. It can only be idealized and beatified in verse or prose by one who knows nothing about it. As a system in practical working, it is a charnel-house of corruption, a whited sepulchre full of dead men's bones.

While the Emperor of China is in person the high-priest of Confucianism, and requires that all office-holders, either in fact or prospect, should conform to that faith, the government is practically tolerant of all forms of religious belief. In the case of Buddhism and Taoism, His Imperial Majesty goes a step further, and patronizes these faiths. He supports a large number of their priests and temples, and on rare occasions visits in state one or more of the latter. But he goes there as a patron, not as a worshiper. He kneels and knocks his head upon the ground at the Temple of Heaven or before the shrine of Confucius, but he merely bows before the image of Buddha or the chief of the many idols that litter his way in a Taoist shrine.

And in the northern and northwestern provinces of China there are millions of Mohammedans, very proud of the fact that they are Persian and not Chinese in origin, who adhere to their own faith and form of worship, yet for centuries have lived unmolested among the Chinese. There are twenty-four Mohammedan mosques in Peking alone.

Strangest of all, in the centre of the province of Honan, which is to say, nearly in the centre of the Chinese Empire, is a single village of Jews, who have manifestly occupied substantially their present location since the dispersion of the tribes. Through all the centuries they have quietly preserved their ancient ritual and all the other essential forms of their national identity.

CHAPTER VII.

CHINESE SUPERSTITIONS.

To any one desirous of studying the effect of superstition upon the human mind, China probably affords a field as choice as any on earth. The entire mental fabric of the nation appears to be saturated with superstitious notions. They play an important part in the daily life of every Chinese, control his plans, whether of business or pleasure, further or thwart his wishes, affect the value of his property, determine whom and when he shall marry, interfere with his relations to his children, sometimes shorten his existence, and always regulate the time, place, and manner of his burial. They pervade all classes, from the highest to the lowest, influence every act in life, distort the reasoning faculties, and make mischief with logic. They are not merely potent in the domestic affairs of private individuals. Grave questions of State, affecting the prosperity if not the very existence of the empire, have in many an instance been decided by them. To a clear-headed foreigner resident in China and associating familiarly with the people, these superstitious notions give an impression as if the entire atmosphere were full of cobwebs, against which he is constantly rushing, sometimes to his amusement and often to his annoyance. But to the Chinese they are no spiders' threads, but unbreakable wires of steel.

In the category of superstitions are included none of the forms or features of either of the Chinese religions which have already been described. They apparently have no connection with religious belief. Were not their influence upon Chinese life so active and decided, one would be inclined to say that they are to religion what fog is to water. But their power is universal, constant, and positive where religion is often only negative. They lack the consistency and symmetrical outlines possessed by even a false religion. They are the vagaries of belief, the isolated, nondescript odds and ends of faith. They are like miscellaneous material left on hand after the completion of a system of supernatural religion, but practically more potent and influential than the system itself. A Chinese will watch complacently the destruction of a mud Buddha, but will refuse to set out on a journey until an astrologer has been consulted and named a lucky day. He will revile all the gods in the Taoist system, and refuse permission to a neighbor to build even a low chimney.

There is one large class of Chinese superstitions that has a sort of topographical character. They relate to locality, and are grouped under the native term as *feng shui*. There fortunately is no English equivalent to this word, since, if we had the word, we should have the thing. It literally means "wind and water," and may be explained sufficiently for our purposes as follows : Each particular spot of ground in the empire has its own spiritual forces or influences. These are inherent in the spot, and are affected by any change in the contour or condition of it, and also by all changes in the circumstances of surrounding localities. Modify in any way or to any extent the environment of a particular plot of ground, and the geomantic forces of the plot are affected for better or worse, but generally, as observation shows, for worse.

These spiritual influences—that is, this *feng shui* —may be friendly to one person and hostile to another. Thus one Chinese may build a house or a place of business upon a particular spot of earth, and the *feng shui* being favorable to him, prosperity will come to him and his ; but if another Chinese should construct the same building, for the same purpose, upon the same location, he would only meet with disaster, because the local influences were hostile to him. His children would die, his business be ruined, and the curse of evil spirits would involve him in hopeless destruction. Upon the other hand, if this second Chinese should construct a different style of building, or the same building for another purpose, the local powers might be satisfied not to annoy him. It may be safe to open a meat market at some spot where the spirits of the locality will not allow dry-goods or hardware to be sold in peace. To take another illustration, Brown may bury his mother in a certain spot and the old lady will rest quietly, her spirit reposing undisturbed and undisturbing in the

TOMB OF THE EMPEROR YUNG LO (DIED A.D. 1425).

coffin. But suppose Smith, instead of Brown, were to bury his mother in the given spot. The old lady might distress and annoy him day and night. Or the mother of either may be quiet there for a while, when something done by Jones in the neighborhood arouses her ire, and her spirit comes forth and allows no one to rest until some action has been taken to quiet her soul and to restore the disturbed *feng shui*. Only a few years since a number of high Chinese officials united in a petition to the throne, asking that a stop be put to mining coal and iron at a point forty miles distant from the imperial tombs, upon the plea that this mining would disturb the bones of the empress, who had recently been buried. A few years earlier the viceroy at Foo Chow formally reported to the Emperor that permission ought not to be granted to certain foreigners to erect buildings upon the slope of a hill within the walls of the city. He based his objection upon the asserted fact that a great dragon rested underneath Foo Chow and supported the foundations of the city; that at the spot named the veins and arteries of the dragon came near to the surface, and hence that the weight of the buildings, if constructed, would impede his circulation.

Tung Chih, the Emperor next preceding the present, died in January, 1875. He was not buried until the following October, as no place could be found in which his remains could be deposited without disturbing the *feng shui*. In order to preserve the balance of spiritual influences, the present dynasty had provided two imperial cemeteries, one about one hundred miles east of Peking, and the other at the same distance to the west. Imperial remains are placed alternately in these abodes of the dead. As Hsein Fêng, the father of Tung Chih, had been buried in the eastern cemetery, the young man himself, according to rule, should have been laid to rest in the western. But the court astrologers declared, as a result of their divinations, that no place could be found there where he might lie without injury to the State, and hence that he must be buried elsewhere. Months of investigation, repeated references to different boards and departments of the public service, and numerous commands from the new Emperor followed, until, after nine months of effort, it was finally decided that he positively could not be interred in the western cemetery, where he belonged, but with certain precautionary and conciliatory measures he might be put under ground in the eastern. This was done as the lesser of two evils. The whole empire had been stirred up over the question; it had been the vital question at numerous councils of State, and a large sum of money, estimated at $250,000, had been expended, all to determine at what spot the remains of a worthless and vicious young man might be put out of sight.

The irreverent person is found in China, as elsewhere, and there were those who asserted in tea-houses and other places of public assemblage that the difficulty was only the result of a combination, a sort of corner on eligible lots, formed by the astrologers. They did not too often have the opportunity of controlling the question of an imperial place of burial, and did not propose to decide the question in this case so long as there was any money to be gained by the creation of difficulties and obstructions. There is, however, no reason to believe that such was the case. If a census of the coffins occupied but unburied within the limits of the empire of China to-day could be taken, the result would be startling. They are more commonly deposited in temples, but are to be found in private houses, in workshops, and are often seen covered by mats in open fields. Lack of time for the elaborate funeral exercises, or of funds to meet the extravagant expenses dictated by custom, is in some instances the cause of the delay, but in a vast majority of cases it is caused by trouble about the *feng shui*. Every family in the country has had its own experience of this sort. The remains must rest, for religious reasons, as shown in another chapter, in the ancestral burying-grounds of the family. The fortune-tellers are invariably consulted upon this and other details of the last rites, and they point out that the spirits interpose certain objections. Then arises a fresh question: By what rearrangement of the ground, change in its contour, or readjustment of surroundings can these objections be removed? In a majority of cases the trouble is easily adjusted, and by some absurdly trivial and inconsequential act, such as the planting of a tree at a particular spot in the cemetery, or perhaps the removal of a shrub or a stone. But in many instances the spirits are obstinate, and the question remains unsolved for months and even years. In the mean time, he would be indeed a brave Chinese who would venture to ignore the *feng shui* and bury his dead. It ought to be said that this delay is not objectionable on the score of health, as might be expected, since Chinese coffins as a rule are hermetically sealed.

Beyond a question, in the enormous class of professional astrologers and diviners in China there are many rapacious frauds. There are quack doctors and disreputable attorneys in the land. But these are exceptions, not the rule. This *feng shui* delusion holds the entire Chinese nation in subjection, and the professors of the art of divination are, as a class, as sincerely its victims as are those who employ them to solve its tangled mysteries in their own affairs. To refer again to the burial of Tung Chih, a large number of the ablest officials of the empire made no effort to conceal their anxiety as to the effect of his being placed in the eastern cemetery. And when, in subsequent years, famine, flood, and other disasters came upon the nation, some of these were bold enough to point out in written memorials to the throne that these calamities came as a result of violated *feng shui*, as punishments for the interment of the late Emperor in a spot where he did not properly belong.

A volume could be written composed entirely of illustrations of the power which this *feng shui*, this topographical superstition, has upon the minds of the nation. It is recognized in the statutes of the empire. A Chinese may sue and recover damages at law against another for any action which can be shown to the satisfaction of the judge to have unfavorably affected the *feng shui* of his house or place of business. A chimney or a window overlooking his premises would at once be accepted as a valid cause of action. And the number of lawsuits based upon this class of complaints is very considerable. Years ago the Secretary of the Chinese Treasury, who was also a celebrated poet, refused to permit a well-known American who resided next door to him, and who was in the service of the Chinese Government, to build any chimneys to his house, as they would affect the *feng shui* of the secretary's residence. In consequence, the American could have no adequate fires in his rooms during the cold winters, and was forced to depend upon charcoal brasiers and outside clothing. Later, the construction of a high chimney for some gas works in the capital reduced by more than one half the value of all structures within a mile of the objectionable work, except such as could be moved away. Church towers and spires are an indiscretion in China, if not a positive menace of danger to those who construct them, since, in the minds of the people, their effect upon the locality is liable to be so injurious in a great variety of supernatural ways.

The effect of such a system upon the lives of those who accept it can hardly be realized. That it must interfere with business, check enterprise, and hamper that individual freedom of action which is essential to healthy development—all this is evident. But it goes far beyond this. It makes men by turns crazy fanatics and senseless cowards. And no cowardice is so damaging and hopeless as that which fears intangible, unseen dangers—dangers which a man cannot struggle against, and from which he cannot run. It can easily be imagined that such a system, with its innumerable ramifications and varieties of application, might absolutely block the wheels of organized social and business life, and bring all things to a standstill. Perhaps it would were not the Chinese remarkable for their capacity of adjustment and for the patience and success with which they manage to evade difficulties and to compromise where they cannot readily conquer. Were they less phlegmatic, good-natured, and practical, the existence of this universal superstition must long since have driven the entire race into lunacy.

They have a great variety of methods of placating the spirits of any locality, of so adjusting and rearranging local influences as to ward off evil and invite good. In any given case the diviner is the man who points out the danger, and he also furnishes the prescription by following which it may be avoided. In passing through the streets of a Chinese city it is not unusual to see, set in the face of a brick wall, a square stone, upon which is cut four characters which read: "This stone, from Mount Tai, is worthy," or, "This stone, from South Mountain, can overcome," as the case may be. The explanation is simple. "Mount Tai" and "South Mountain" are two famous sacred spots in China. Stones from them have been brought, often at no slight expense, cut as described, and set into walls at particular points as a prescribed corrective of some imaginary evil influences. They are more commonly seen placed in the wall of a building exactly opposite the end of a street which opens into but does not cross the street on which the building stands. In such case the theory is that they will cause any evil spirits or

PAGODA AT YU CHUAN SHAN (IMPERIAL SUMMER PALACE).

influences which may come down this street to turn at right angles and proceed, whereas but for the presence of these sacred stones they would penetrate the wall and work mischief to the inmates of the building. Another simple and inexpensive method of securing good fortune is to write upon a strip of red paper four Chinese characters which mean, "May he opposite me receive happiness," or, "May he opposite me secure wealth." Thus written, the slip is posted on the wall *opposite* to the main entrance to the residence or office of him for whose benefit it is intended. As the word "me" in either sentence refers to the slip of paper itself, it will at once be seen to apply to the Chinese across the street, by whom it was posted.

A considerable number of the pagodas which add beauty to the Chinese landscape have been constructed with a view to the permanent adjustment of these spiritual influences. The Chinese appear to believe in "luck in odd numbers," since they must always contain an odd number of stories. That here reproduced is one of the most beautiful in the empire. It is built upon the summit of "The Hill of the Jade Fountain," in the enclosure of the Summer Palace, about eight miles west of Peking.

Small shrines are also built for this same object at prescribed points. These are seen upon the roofs of houses in every city. In such cases they are only suitable for sparrows' nests in point of size, and are put in place to correct some disturbance of the *feng shui*. Far more pretentious structures have been built upon river-banks by imperial command to placate the local deity, the "river dragon," who in some fit of anger, or possibly in order to attract attention, had undermined a dyke, or in some other way caused a flood and thus devastated the surrounding country.

There are innumerable forms of supernatural influences courted or feared by the Chinese other than that known as *feng shui*. There are fortunate and unfortunate times and seasons. If land is to be purchased, a lucky day must be discovered upon which the transfer may be made. If a new house is to be occupied, the family can safely enter it only upon a lucky day. If a merchant is to open a new place of business or an official take up a new post of duty, the one may open his store and the other take the seals of office only upon a lucky day. The dates of weddings and funerals are invariably fixed in the same way. The diviner is consulted, furnished with certain data, and with these as a basis, a routine of hocus-pocus is gone through with and a suitable date announced. In the case of a prospective wedding, the fortune-teller goes a step further. He is given two slips of paper containing the family and given names of the two matrimonial candidates, the year, month, day, and hour of the birth of each, and from these he determines whether a matrimonial alliance between them would be fortunate. If he decides in the negative, the scheme is dropped at once. There is no thought of appeal from his judgment, and no Chinese would be bold enough to marry in the face of it. As there is never any affection existing between the two persons, the abandonment of the alliance involves no sorrow.

There are many varieties of Chinese geomancy. Space will not allow a description of them, nor are they of sufficient interest or peculiarity to warrant it. It is enough to remark, in passing, that in some of their features they bear a very close family resemblance to similar methods of learning or forecasting the future and the decrees of fate which were in vogue in Europe more than a century ago. Neither Asiatic nor European may have borrowed from the other. They either came from a common original source, or their strong resemblance shows that the human intellect is essentially the same throughout the earth.

Times of distress appear to bring to the surface the superstitious ideas of the Chinese, much as they are said to develop the religious feeling of nominal Christians. In seasons of drought the inhabitants of Peking go by tens of thousands to a particular spot in the old Mongol wall of the city, several miles outside of the present enclosure, and there burn incense and pray for rain at an abandoned fox-hole. They literally pray to the hole, and not to the fox. His ancestors doubtless misunderstood the devotional tendencies of their visitors—perhaps thought that they came for blood rather than water—and hence moved away generations ago.

This may seem a traveler's fox story, but it is a fact. The course of the Imperial Government in times of lack of rain is not far removed from it in absurdity, and may render the conduct of the populace more credible. In such times of distress the first act of the Emperor is to prohibit the killing of beef. I have never been able to secure an intelligent explanation of this act. It probably has some connection with the fact that bullocks are offered as sacrifices upon the altar of Heaven, and hence are supposed to have a semi-sacred character. This measure failing to produce rain, the Emperor goes to the altar just mentioned, and there, on behalf of himself and the nation, sacrifices to Heaven and prays for rain. If relief fails to come, he may repeat the sacrifice and prayer, and possibly go a third time. But if his prayers at the Temple of Heaven prove unavailing, he resorts to extreme measures. Several hundred years ago a piece of iron was found in a well in a temple enclosure several hundred miles to the southwest of Peking. It was declared to have dropped into the well from Heaven, and has since been kept as a sacred relic in the temple. The Emperor sends a commission headed by an imperial prince to the temple to receive this bit of rusty iron from the priests and carry it to the capital. There it is deposited with elaborate ceremonies in a temple, and on a day named in advance by proclamation, the Emperor proceeds to this temple, prostrates himself before the bit of iron, and prays to it for rain.

It is not often that the spirits which, in his imagination, fill the atmosphere about every Chinese, which he fears and consults—it is not often that they are shaped by his hands into visible forms and worshiped in temples. Occasionally he does, however, find an object of worship ready-made by nature, and he makes haste to propitiate and court its favor by offerings and prayers. Thus a little south of the centre of the province of Shan Hsi is a city called Ling Shih Hsien (the City of the Spiritual Stone). Within the walls of the city is the

"Temple of the Spiritual Stone," a small but beautiful and well-kept temple, with a staff of priests, sleek, well fed, and manifestly well cared for. I visited it in 1874 and saw this "Spiritual Stone," which has been worshiped for centuries, and which has not only its shrine and staff of servitors, but has given a name to a city and a district in the government of China. It is a dark-colored stone, some four or five feet in diameter, of a spherical shape, yet quite irregular in outline, worn smooth and glossy by the kissing of many generations. The most wonderful stories were poured into my ears regarding its power and kindly disposition by the priests who attended me. I was invited to believe that before me at last lay the potent source of all good, and the sure guard against evil. It was a panacea for all diseases, a balm for every sorrow. Near it lay a small hammer, and the skeptical were allowed to strike the stone and thus prove its spiritual qualities. Having expressed my doubts of this curious divinity to the priests, the hammer was given me, and I was invited to use it and prove whether his spiritual highness would respond. I did so, and gave the stone a rather sharp rap, when a clear, bell-like tone was heard in response. The priests were triumphant, and I was entirely convinced that their wonderful rock god was either a meteorolite or a fine specimen of native iron ore which abounds in that section of the country.

In a similar way peculiar spiritual powers are sometimes supposed to exist in old trees. Altars are erected in front of them, and the trunk and limbs are hung thick with native offerings. These consist mainly of bits of board upon which are written sentences of praise for the virtues which the tree is supposed to possess, and the benefits derived from prayer to it. I saw many such in a long journey made in 1874. I saw one standing in a wheat field about five miles from the capital of the province of Shan Hsi, a gnarled, weather-beaten locust, evidently hundreds of years of age. The natives insisted that it dated back to the Yao dynasty, which would make it more than four thousand years old. While making all due allowance for devotional exaggeration, it may be said that this locust has a wide reputation, not merely for its spiritual properties, but as being the oldest and most venerable tree in the empire. It has been worshiped for many generations. When I saw it it was quite overburdened with tablets of all sorts, containing such inscriptions as " Praise for benefits received," " Thanks for healing mercies," " Ask and ye shall receive," etc. It had a special reputation for curing diseases of the eye, and, in consequence, viewed at a distance, it resembled a ragged beggar, covered as it was with strips of cloth upon which a pair of eyes had been painted. These had been prepared by those whose vision had, as they believed, been improved by a pilgrimage to the tree, one end of the cloth being nailed to it, and the strip left to sway and flutter in the wind.

There are an immense variety of whimsical and amusing superstitions touching nearly every event in the ordinary life of the Chinese, yet less important than those described. No person of the female sex is allowed, under any circumstances, to approach a well that is in the process of being dug. A red flag is hoisted when the first spadeful of earth is removed, and that flag is the warning for all females to keep their distance. I could never discover the *rationale* of this practice. No matter how formal or prolonged a dinner may be—and I have attended one consisting of seventy-eight courses and lasting twelve hours—the Chinese do not allow the plates of any persons at the table to be changed from the beginning of the feast to the end. On one occasion, being the guest of honor at a dinner in the most fashionable restaurant of Peking, my host, who was a high official as well as an intimate friend, remarked: "I have been your guest and you have been mine many times. We each understand well the customs of the other. I have noticed at foreign tables that the plates are removed and clean ones placed after each course. You have undoubtedly noticed that we never change ours. Do you know the reason why we require our guests to use the same plate from the beginning of a feast to the end?" As I had always supposed that the only reason was a lack of tidiness on the part of the Chinese, but, in politeness, could not say so, I found it more convenient to reply that I did not know. My host appeared to read my thoughts, for he continued: "You may have charged it to untidiness, but that is not the explanation. We have a very old superstition, which is expressed in the saying, 'Huan Chia huo sz hsi fu erh'" ("Change the plates and the

CHINESE CATAFALQUE.

housewife will die"). These are given as samples of an unnumbered host.

No sketch of the superstitions current among the Chinese would be just and accurate if it failed to include the darker shades of the picture, or, in other words, to point out the inhuman conduct and horrible cruelty which follow them as an inevitable result. Enough has already been said in these pages to show that family affection has at least a normal degree of development among the Chinese. They are not lacking in regard for those who are related to them by ties of blood. On the contrary, they make a boast of their love of kindred, and the most offensive and disgraceful adjective they can apply to an enemy is one implying that he is lacking in this regard. Yet never, if it can possibly be avoided, will they allow a relative, no matter how near and dear he may be, to die quietly in bed. At the last moment, perhaps at the instant when life is passing from the body, it must be removed from the bed and stretched upon a board. When sufficient warning is given of approaching dissolution, this is done with the utmost gentleness and care. But at all costs it must be done before life is extinct, and hence is often effected with such haste and inevitable harshness as to increase suffering, if not to hasten the end. This course is the result of a superstition that if a person dies in bed his soul takes possession of and remains in the bed, and renders both it and the room uninhabitable by other persons. In all cases where death occurs before this removal has been effected, the bed must be torn down and destroyed and the entire room renovated before it can again be used.

Charges of infanticide have, from the beginning of our knowledge of the Chinese, been brought against them. Intelligent foreigners, long resident in the empire, have positively insisted that it was a common practice. Others, equally reliable and well qualified to speak upon the subject, have with equal earnestness denied its existence. Dr. S. Wells Williams, than whom no more competent and careful authority exists, says of the practice in Southern China: " Investigations have been made about Canton and evidence obtained to show that it is comparatively rare, and not at all countenanced by public opinion, though by no means unknown nor punished by law when done." There certainly is no evidence to show that it is, in any fair meaning of the word, a practice in the northern parts of the empire.

But a foreigner resident in, say, Peking, if he be of an observant disposition, will soon be struck with one strange fact. He sees an abundance of children playing about the streets, of all ages and sizes. He can readily see, from the manner of life of the people and the entire absence of trained physicians, that the death-rate among the young must be at least as great as in any Western city; yet he never sees a child's funeral. He will puzzle over this problem for a time, perhaps ask an explanation from a native friend, and receive no satisfactory answer, since it is both impolite and unlucky in Chinese ideas to discuss such a topic. Then, if he happens to be upon the street very early some morning, he will find the hideous explanation of his puzzle. He will meet, as I have many a time, the dead cart, a large covered vehicle drawn by two oxen, having a sign across the front stating its horrible office, and piled to the brim with the bodies of children. I have seen at least a hundred in the cart at once, thrown in as garbage, nearly all of them naked, a few tied up in old reed baskets, and fewer—never more than one or two—in cheap board coffins. These carts go about the streets each night, pick up these pitiable remains, some of them mutilated by dogs; they are thrown in like so much wood, and taken to a pit outside of the city walls, into which they are dumped and there covered with quicklime. Small wonder that a theory of infanticide was deemed necessary to account for such an unutterably hideous custom!

And yet, so far at least as North China is concerned, these unfortunate bits of humanity are seldom the victims of *intentional* infanticide; but they are the victims of one of the most cruel and revolting superstitions that ever found lodgment in a human brain. When a child sickens, it has, according to the means and intelligence of the parents, the same anxious care and medical attendance that would be given among us; but if all remedies fail of effect, and death is apparently near, the situation changes at once. The little thing is stripped naked and placed on the floor, which is either of mud or brick, just inside the outer door of the room. The parents leave it there, and watch the issue. If, which is seldom the case, it survives the ordeal, it is a true child of their own flesh and blood; if it dies, then it never was their child, but an evil spirit seeking admission to their hearthstone in order to work them mischief and ruin. Hence, it is thrown into the street to be gathered up by the dead-cart, as already described. No power could induce them to give it proper burial in the family resting-place for the dead. That would mean its adoption by them, and what sane Chinese would adopt an evil spirit into his family? This is the theory, and this the way they argue and act; and the dead-cart, with its freight, is the fearful result. Evidently such treatment kills many young children who under other circumstances would recover, and the results of this superstition are great enough to fully account for a theory of willful infanticide.

This theory and line of conduct is common to all classes of the Chinese. The military governor of Peking, an officer of the highest rank and a man of unusual intelligence, was granted leave for a number of weeks. While still absent from duty, he called upon me one afternoon. I was shocked at his wretched appearance, and inquired if he had been ill. His reply is given in his own words: "No, I have not been ill, but have seen a great deal of trouble. I have been married many years, and have several daughters. You know how anxious we Chinese are for male offspring, and so can imagine how proud and happy I was when, three years ago, a son was born to me. He was a rugged, bright boy, and never ill a day until about two months ago, when he began to pine. I called our native physicians, but he grew worse, and at last, about two weeks ago, as a last resort, I called one of your foreign doctors. You can conceive how anxious I was that he should live by my consent to that; but he could not help the little fellow, and *one night last week I was obliged to throw his body outside the door.*"

Another case came even more directly under my personal knowledge. A young missionary lady went earlier than usual one Sunday morning to the Chinese chapel, in order to have time before the service to inquire after the grandson of the chapel-keeper or janitor, who, she had been told, was ill. There was an obstruction against the door of the janitor's room, but she managed to enter, and saw, lying on the mud floor of the room, and partly against the door, the naked body of the little boy after whose health she wished to inquire. The parents and grandparents sat the farther side of the room, showing deep grief, but making no effort for the dying child. There was no fire in the room, though it was late in November, and a raw, cold wind blew through many holes in the paper windows. With a scream of horror the young lady snatched her shawl from her shoulders, wrapped the little body in it, and tried to bring back the nearly departed breath. She sent the father for hot water, had a fire made, and at last succeeded in restoring some semblance of life. Then, leaving strict charge to keep the child well wrapped in her shawl and near the fire, and seeing no reason to fear that the little fellow would die, she went into church. Returning after an hour, she found the same obstruction against the door, and this time she came too late. The child was too far gone to be called back to life, and died in her arms. The instant she left the room to attend service it had again been stripped and placed upon the floor, in order to determine whether it was a true child or a fiend. No threats or persuasions could move the parents to give it burial in the family cemetery. They at last consented to place it in a cheap coffin, carry it out of the city at dawn, and bury it in some field.

This was an only child. The parents and grandparents were Christians, and had for years lived lives consistent with their profession. In no other way did they subsequently show themselves unfit to be regarded as such. It is necessary to state these facts in order to show what a terrible grip this fearful superstition has upon the Chinese mind.

CHAPTER VIII.

CHINESE QUEUES.

One of the most marked and striking points of difference between Oriental and Western races is found in the hair. Oriental hair is always coarse, straight, and a true jet black. That of the people of Europe and America is softer, silkier, often inclined to curl, and of every variety of coloring, except the dead black of the raven's wing. That is rarely found. In many years of residence in the East I have never seen upon the head of a pure-blooded Chinese, Japanese, Corean, Mongolian, Manchu, Malay, or Indian any other shade of hair than black, excepting, of course, those heads on which age had bleached the covering to gray or white, and one family of Chinese Albinos, whose eyes were pink and whose hair was like driven snow in color.

Another and equally marked point of difference is found in the growth of hair upon the face. No amount of coaxing or cultivation ever yet enabled an Asiatic to grow more than a most scanty beard or mustache. At the most one may see a Chinese or other Oriental with a few straggling hairs upon his chin or upper lip, or what is more common, an utter absence of mustache and whiskers, with three or four long hairs growing from a mole on his cheek or chin. For these the proud possessor carries a special comb, and they are combed, fingered,

PEDDLING FRUIT.

and generally cared for with the utmost attention, as precious, if scanty, signs of manhood.

The foreigner's whiskers form the one mark of beauty which makes him an object of envy to his Chinese neighbors. They do not admire the color of his hair, nor admit that, short and bushy as it is, it at all compares with their glossy, straight braids. They vote his large nose ugly, dislike his pale complexion, criticise the color of his eyes, and object to the angle at which they are set. They draw unfriendly comparisons between his ears and those found on their donkeys; but in the matter of whiskers they regard him as, indeed, highly favored of Heaven.

Many of them do not limit their idea of the capacity of foreigners to develop beard and whiskers to one sex. In the autumn of 1874 I traveled for several months in the far interior of China, where foreigners had seldom if ever been seen, with two American gentlemen as companions. One of these was exceedingly short of stature and slight, but he had all the marks of manhood about him, including a distinctively piercing male eye and an abundant beard, which reached well down over his chest. To our surprise, and the unmeasured disgust of the victim of Chinese misunderstanding, this gentleman during a large part of our travels was taken by the Chinese to be a woman, and my wife. It is impossible to explain the absurd mistake, except upon the ground of his very slight figure and small stature. In one city of perhaps one hundred thousand people, all of whom apparently came to stare at us, I overheard the following conversation between two of the well-to-do residents of the place. Said Ah Hsin, pointing to my companion, who was standing near me on the street: "That is a woman." "Impossible," returned the other; "only look at his beard." "Ugh!" grunted Ah Hsin, "you don't know much. In their country the women have beards exactly the same as the men." Doubting Thomas gave vent to an ejaculation of astonishment at the fact and of admiration at the broad range of his neighbor's information, and the conversation ended.

The queue is more than the badge or mark of a Chinese, it is the symbol of Chinese manhood. In infancy and childhood the head is either clean shaven and kept as smooth and shining as a billiard-ball, or patches of hair are left to grow in circles, helter-skelter, upon its surface, and from each arises a little tuft or braid, as though the blood, in an excess of vitality, was sending out the sprouts of half-a-dozen queues. It is only when the boy reaches the age of thirteen or fourteen that these "baby sprouts" are shaved off, and he is formally invested with the sober and dignified queue of manhood.

But the queue, although the symbol of Chinese manhood, is not originally Chinese. It is a foreign importation, and compared with other fashions in the empire, is a modern and recent innovation. It is Tartar or Mongolian, and was introduced only about three hundred years ago by the present ruling family, which is itself foreign. It may be added, in passing, that this style of dressing the hair is about the only thing adopted by the Chinese from the Manchus. Prior to the present dynasty, the Chinese did not shave the head, and dressed their hair much as we do ours. When the throne was seized by the ancestor of the present ruler, a decree was issued by the new Emperor commanding all good subjects to shave the head and adopt the queue. This at once aroused intense excite-

GROUP OF CHILDREN.

ment and bitter opposition throughout the empire. To wear the queue was held to be degrading, and a badge of slavery to a foreign tyrant. Mobs and riots occurred, for a time there was much trouble, and it appeared doubtful if the new fashion could be enforced without another long and bloody war.

The Tartar Emperor was, however, equal to the occasion, and met the difficulty with that shrewdness and tact which has made his name historical in China as the wisest of all her rulers, ancient or modern. He indulged in no threats, attempted no coercion; he quietly ignored the opposition, and issued a further decree by which he forbade persons convicted of crime to wear the queue, requiring his officers to cut off this appendage from all such persons, and not to allow them to shave their heads. He thus made a shaven head and a queue a mark of respectability, and his new subjects were soon as eager to adopt the new mode of dressing the hair as they had been determined in opposition to it. To this day a full head of hair and the absence of a queue are in China the badge of a criminal. The Manchu Emperor went a step further, and called to his aid the intense devotion of the Chinese to the doctrine of filial piety. He prescribed an unshaven head and a disheveled, uncombed queue as one of the badges of mourning the death of a parent. For a period of one hundred days from such a loss no dutiful son will call in the services of a barber or allow his hair to be arranged, no matter how slovenly in appearance it may become.

The queue has now become an object of almost superstitious reverence among the Chinese. It is combed and dressed with the greatest care, enlarged and lengthened with horsehair or silk, wound about the head at times, and neatly covered to protect it from the dust. It is universally treated as an object of dignity and honor. The Chinese boy longs for it as the American boy longs for trousers with pockets in them. To pull it is an insult and to cut it off a grave offense, severely punishable by law.

The etiquette of the queue is as exacting and particular as that of any other portion of the costume or the manners of the Oriental. It is the mark of a rowdy to wear it loosely braided. The strands must be drawn tight and snug. It is ordinarily bound with a black silk cord and tassel at the end, but—white being the Chinese mourning color—when a Chinese is in mourning, the black cord must be exchanged for a white one. If a person, traveling upon a dusty road, has coiled and wrapped up his queue to keep it clean, and thus meets a friend or acquaintance, he must, before recognizing or addressing him, sweep the queue down from its coil and see that it hangs behind him in a straight, decorous fashion. Under a similar rule of propriety no servant may be allowed to appear in the presence of his master or mistress with his queue coiled. It would be considered as serious an act of rudeness as if he came half dressed.

Such and so intense being the regard of the Chinese for this national mode of dressing the

CHINESE BARBER.

hair, it is not surprising to one who knows their intensely superstitious temperament that nearly every year, in some section of the empire, a perfect whirlwind of excitement should suddenly spring up with no apparent cause over what is commonly called "tail-cutting." As a rule, no one knows how it began, what occasioned it, or how it may end. It comes and goes as unexpectedly and with as little warning as the cyclone upon a Western prairie. In some instances, however, it has been willfully aroused by malicious Chinese of the educated class to gratify their hatred of foreigners, and in such cases care is taken, of course, to direct suspicion against them as the authors of the mischief. More than once in recent years the lives of unoffending foreigners have been placed in actual peril by such absurd reports.

In such a fever, the entire mass of the population, the most intelligent as well as the most ignorant, go wild with excitement and fear. The absurdest stories are circulated and believed. Here are samples, taken from the actual experience of the writer. Such a Chinese was walking along the street when his queue suddenly dropped off and vanished. No human being was near him at the time. Such another man put up his hand to coil his queue, and discovered that he had none. Such another experienced a sensation of cold in the back of his neck, and thus discovered that his queue had departed. This man fell into conversation with a stranger upon the street, who suddenly vanished, and the man's queue followed. Another glanced at a foreign child, when the child gazed steadily at him, and his queue at once faded out of sight, leaving only an odor of burnt hair.

These are specimens of the stories told everywhere in times of this excitement, and universally believed. Argument or appeal to common sense are utterly useless. It is idle to reason that hair can only be cut by shears or a similarly sharp instrument, which must be operated by human hands. The Chinese believe implicitly in magic arts and evil spirits, and, as these specimen stories show, they credit much if not all of the " tail-cutting" to such influences. Indeed, it is wiser for foreigners in such periods of frenzy not to attempt argument even with their most familiar Oriental friends or servants, but rather to preserve a discreet silence upon the subject. One never knows in such times whether a thoughtless word upon the subject may not direct suspicion against the speaker, nor what the consequences of such a word may be.

It would naturally be expected that, in such mental typhoons, the officials would concert measures to suppress the excitement and reassure the populace. They do nothing of the sort. In all matters of superstition or belief in magic they are hardly more enlightened than those whom they govern. I have seen, first and last, at least a dozen proclamations, issued by magistrates of Peking, in times of this sort of excitement, and every one was directly calculated to increase rather than lessen the disturbance of the public mind. They commonly began by warning the people that these were days of danger, when every person should stay closely at home and attend to his own affairs. They advised all to avoid strangers, see that their doors and windows were carefully closed at all hours, on no account to be out after dark, and to look after their children. Some of them concluded by furnishing a sovereign protection, a sort of patent-medicine recipe for securing the queue from harm. This recipe in most cases was very simple. In one proclamation it merely directed that a red and yellow cord be braided in with the hair; in another it prescribed a medicine to be taken internally, and in another, which also prescribed a medicine, one half was to be swallowed and the other half thrown upon the kitchen fire.

One of these prescriptions, which I well remember, was issued by the mayor of Peking in January, 1877. It directed that a sort of monogram, composed of three Chinese characters intertwined in a certain manner, should be written in black ink upon three squares of a fixed size of a peculiar yellow paper. One of these squares must be burned, the ashes carefully saved and swallowed in a cup of tea; the second must be worn braided into the strands of the queue; and the third must be pasted upon the outside of the door-frame, exactly over the centre of the door. Thus defended, the mayor assured his people that they might rest safely and defy the malignant spirits that roamed about day and night, seeking opportunities to rob the faithful Sons of Han of their badges of manhood and nationality. The prescription was modestly styled " The Universal and Infallible Queue Protector."

It should be added that in none of these "tail-cutting excitements" was there the least tangible evidence that even one Chinese had suffered the loss of a single hair from his head. Every man's mouth was full of stories such as have been described, the people were utterly demoralized, business was at a standstill, and yet not one curtailed Chinese could be produced. Those who, with bated breath and frightened face, related the various instances, had seen none of them, their informants had seen none; and, in fact, in all these troubles I never saw a Chinese who had seen another who had lost his queue in any such inexplicable manner. The basis of every one of the stories was hearsay; and each such excitement was an unaccountable but dangerous epidemic of superstitious fear.

During the height of such a fever in Peking, and shortly after the mayor had issued his proclamation and prescription, as given above, I was called from bed early one morning to see an American missionary, who came to report that during the preceding night a Chinese, while sleeping in the chapel under his charge, had been deprived of his queue. Knowing well that, in the excitement then raging, if a rumor of the fact got abroad the chapel would be destroyed in an hour by a howling mob, and perhaps human lives be lost, the missionary had, with great prudence, locked the sufferer in a room by himself, and hurried at daybreak to the Legation for advice and assistance. Having sent a hasty note to the military governor of the city asking for an interview at a later hour in the day, giving no reason for the request, but the object being to secure, if necessary, a body of soldiers to guard the chapel from a mob, I went to the spot to investigate the affair.

The facts were very simple. It was an actual case of " tail-cutting," the first and last that I ever saw, except in numerous instances where criminals had been deprived of their queues under due process of law. The despoiled Chinese was a " man from the country," who had come to Peking to study Christianity, and who had been kindly allowed by the missionary to remain for a few days and nights with two native Christians in a small room at the back of the chapel building. As he was a stranger, it was at least possible that he had been sent by malicious Chinese to the chapel, and having secured a footing there under pretense of interest in Christianity, had cut off his own queue, hoping in this way to raise a disturbance against foreigners ; but under the closest questioning he told a perfectly straight and consistent story, and this suspicion was abandoned.

He had gone to bed the evening before, in the room where I found him, at nine o'clock, and the other two men had followed him shortly after. He awoke at about two in the morning, and, feeling queer about his head, put up his hand and found his queue gone. Frightened nearly out of his wits, he cried out and awoke his companions, who, not less alarmed than he, lighted a candle, and the three sat up and trembled until nearly daybreak, when one of them called the missionary. On going out for this purpose he found the missing queue on the snow in the yard, where it had evidently been thrown.

Such were the facts developed by close questions. It puzzled me greatly. The two men who were in the room through the night with the countryman were well known, and above suspicion. They confirmed his statement so far as they knew anything about the affair. The yard where the queue was found was surrounded by a high wall which could not be scaled. The doors and windows of the room had been carefully fastened the evening before, and no one could have entered without the knowledge of the occupants. The queue had been cut off. That was evident. There it was in my hand. It had been cut with shears, about an inch from the head, with a single clean, sharp stroke. It was unusually thick, and must have required a strong wrist, keen shears, and great caution to have severed it from the head without disturbing its owner.

After a long investigation, devoid of the least result, I asked, as I had many times before:

"Was there no person but you three in the room at bedtime?"

"No."

"Was there no one else here earlier in the evening?"

One said "No," but another, after a moment's thought, said: "Yes, early in the evening Ah Hsin [not his real name] was here, but he left before we went to bed."

"What was he doing?"

"He was fastening some foreign paper together into a book."

"What tools had he?"

"Some twine, a needle, and a pair of shears."

"Were there, or had there been recently, another pair of shears in the room?"

"No, not for a long time."

"Did Ah Hsin take the shears away with him?"

"Yes."

Further questions brought out the facts that Ah Hsin did not leave the room until after the countryman was in bed and asleep, and that he sat at his work of bookbinding in such a position that the head of the sleeper was close at his right hand, while the other two Chinese were at some distance, on the other side of a table, busily engaged in reading. Under these circumstances nothing could have been more easy than for Ah Hsin, without even turning his body, to have seized the queue of the sleeper and cut it off with his shears without attracting the attention of the others. If either of them chanced to look up at the critical moment, the table, being considerably higher than the head of the victim, would have screened the operation from his view.

Ah Hsin had formerly been in the service of a friend. I had known of him as a young Chinese scapegrace, equally handsome and mischievous, and hence had little doubt that he could explain this tail-cutting episode if he chose. The missionary was, therefore, requested to go in person for Ah Hsin, who was employed in a printing-office connected with the mission establishment, and to bring him at once before me, with no hint as to the purpose for which he was wanted. Ah Hsin soon appeared, bright-faced, frank, and smiling, and, having made the usual salutation, calmly stood awaiting my pleasure. Without prelude of any sort, I asked him why he had cut off the countryman's queue the previous evening. He stoutly denied having done so, showed natural astonishment at the fact that it had been cut, and wondered who could have been guilty of the act. He admitted having been in the room, having shears, and having been seated as the others had described. Under close questioning he confessed that the paper which he had been sewing into book form had been stolen by him from the printing-office. That, he said, was a small affair, stealing a ream or two of paper, but to cut off a Chinese queue was a very serious matter, deserving heavy punishment, and he never, never could have been guilty of such an act.

Thus he answered all questions for more than an hour. It was impossible to trip him at any point. He was more profoundly impressed with the gravity of the offense than I was. Blandishment and persuasion could not move or trap him. When I assured him, for example, that of course it was plain that he meant no harm, but only used the shears as a boyish freak, overcome by temptation for a lark, when he saw the sleeping man's queue hanging over the edge of the bed so conveniently, he corrected me at once. He was a Chinese himself, and knew better than to meddle with a man's queue, even in sport. Whoever cut that tail, cut it not in mischief. It was a serious business. Assurances that no harm should come to him if he confessed had no effect. As he had not done the deed, how could he confess?

It is easy in this way to recite the general substance of the conversation, and to show its utter failure; but neither pen nor pencil could paint the innocent, boyish face, the calm, quiet eye, the ready, positive, but courteous tones of his voice, and, in general, the absolute lack of any trace of guilt. If Ah Hsin was guilty, then all signs fail with the Chinese, as they sometimes do. A friend, who was remarkably successful in detecting Chinese thieves, once stated that his secret lay wholly in suddenly asking the suspected person the question why or when he stole the missing articles, and then closely watching his throat. If he was guilty, he invariably *swallowed* before making reply. But Ah Hsin did not even swallow.

At last, wearied and out of patience, yet fully convinced that he cut the queue, I said: " Very well. You deny the act. I am none the less certain that you are guilty. I came here and sent for you, not to get you into trouble, but to help you out of it. I have no desire to see you punished, and, as I have repeatedly assured you, would gladly do any possible thing to save you from it. You are guilty. You cut that queue. You know better than I do what the Chinese officials will do in these days of excitement with any person who is even suspected of tail-cutting. That queue was cut last evening in this room with a pair of shears. You were in the room, had the only pair of shears in it, and, by your own admission, they did not pass out of your possession the entire evening. I shall hand you over to the Chinese authorities with a statement of the facts, and leave them to decide, as is their duty, whether you are innocent or guilty."

Even this did not move him. So, turning to a servant who had accompanied me, I directed him to take my card to a police station near at hand, and ask that two officers be sent to me at once. Ah Hsin heard this, still he stood with apparent unconcern until the servant was passing through the door, when, quick as a flash, his manner changed, and he said :

"You need not do that. You were quite correct. I did cut off the queue after the man was asleep, and exactly as you supposed, and dropped it on the snow outside the door when I went home. I did it to plague and frighten him, he is such a very green countryman."

Knowing how little mercy the boy would receive for his thoughtless act at the hands of the native authorities, I agreed with the missionary not to report the case to them, but to make some excuse for the request for an interview with the military governor. The missionary promised, on his part, to send Ah Hsin out of the city without an hour's delay, and to keep the curtailed countryman in solitary confinement for the day; then he, too, was to be escorted out of town by two discreet Chinese and sent home with a small present. This plan was successfully carried out, and no hint of the one genuine case of tail-cutting got abroad.

The sequel to this incident will illustrate how seriously the highest officials in China regard the offense of tail-cutting. A week later, Prince Kung, then Prince Regent of the empire, came to the Legation with the members of the Cabinet to make a New Year's call. In the course of conversation he inquired what I wished of the military governor that day when I first asked to see him, and then withdrew the request. It appeared that they had only found him with much difficulty, and had but just notified him of my appointment when it was canceled by the second note. In reply I recited the facts of the case, adding that the queue was cut off in a mere boyish freak, which it had seemed best to overlook; but the prince failed to view it in that light. He became much excited, said that the Chinese boy knew well what he was about when he cut off the queue, that he had forfeited his life, and insisted upon being furnished with his name and place of residence. Fortunately I did not know either Ah Hsin's family name or where he had been sent, and hence was unable to put the authorities upon his trail. There is little doubt that the boyish freak would have cost him his life had he fallen into their hands at that time.

CHAPTER IX.

CHINESE COURTS OF LAW.

In the centre of the main entrance to the official residence of every Chinese magistrate is a low wooden platform, about ten feet square, carpeted with red felt. Upon this are placed a table and an imposing magisterial chair, both draped in red. Upon the table are writing materials, while on the wall near at hand hang whips, bamboo rods, and other instruments of punishment. At one side of the platform are suspended a gong and a bell, with the usual wooden hammer for beating either of them.

This constitutes the primitive Chinese hall of justice, and is an arrangement as old as the empire. While practically all cases are tried within walls and many behind closed doors, yet theoretically this remains the court, public to all who may come and open to Heaven. Any Chinese subject having a complaint against another may come at any hour of the day or night and beat the gong. Thereupon the magistrate is bound by law to put on instantly his official robes, come forth, seat himself in the chair of judgment, and then and there, in the presence of whoever may choose to be present, to hear and determine the case without fear, favor, fee, or reward. This is the Chinese exemplification of the old saying that "the eye of justice never sleeps." In theory, at least, Chinese justice is speedy, inexpensive, and sure.

The judicial system of China is probably the oldest in the world, and appears to have undergone no serious changes in many centuries. It is simple, and bears evidence of careful effort to protect all who have occasion to use it, whether as accusing or accused, against injustice or extortion. Numerous checks, such as appeals to higher courts, and a final revision by the Emperor himself, are provided in certain cases. There is one system of courts, established at an early day in the history of the empire, especially intended for the protection of the very poor, and in which no fees or expenses of any sort could be exacted under any excuse or pretext. The meanest beggar may, by taking the prescribed steps, be assured in theory that his cause will come before His Imperial Majesty in person, and judgment be entered upon it by nothing less august and final than the "vermilion pencil."

This last-named court, or system of courts, is unique in its organization and range of duty. It is known in Chinese as the "Tu Cha Yuan," or "The Metropolitan Department of Investigation." The title is ordinarily translated as "The Censorate," which substantially indicates its duties. These are to hear all judicial cases which may be brought to its notice absolutely without tax, fee, or compensation of any sort, and to review, examine, and criticise the conduct of all officials of every rank, grade, or duty in the empire. Not an individual, no matter what his position, is either too high or too low to be free from the scrutiny of the officers of this department. The Emperor himself is often censured by them. When Kuang Hsu, the present occupant of the throne, was on his way

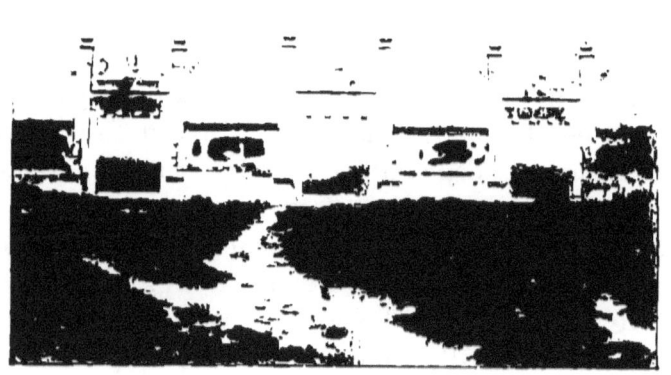

ENTRANCE TO IMPERIAL CEMETERY.

to attend the funeral of the preceding emperor, a censor placed in his hands a report protesting against his accession to imperial power, and then, to mark the earnestness of his conviction, took his own life in the presence of the new monarch, who was a mere child, three years of age. In 1871 a censor in Peking boldly defied Prince Kung, who was then at the head of affairs, and the latter found it more safe to violate his own word, pledged to the American Minister, than to undertake the task of controlling a native official who was very much below him in rank.

The code of laws, which dates back twenty centuries, and is revised frequently, is, as has been pointed out in another chapter, upon the whole wise, moderate, and humane. It prescribes, with great minutiæ, various kinds and grades of punish-

APPROACH TO MING TOMBS.

ment for the varying circumstances of crime. It provides for an increasing severity of punishment for repetitions of a given offense, in much the same manner as our own laws. A large number of minor penalties may be legally compromised by the payment of a fine. Thus an offender sentenced to receive a hundred blows may avoid the penalty by the payment of five ounces of silver. Other provisions are more humane than would be expected. Thus, if any criminal under sentence of death has parents or grandparents who are infirm or above the age of seventy, and who have no other son or grandson to care for them, his case must be brought to the notice of His Imperial Majesty. Women who are sentenced to receive a flogging must be allowed to retain their under-garments when the punishment is inflicted, and no punishment, except for treason or rebellion, can be visited upon persons under seven and over ninety years of age. Some of the provisions of the code are amusing and grotesque. Thus, astronomers who have been sentenced to banishment may submit to a hundred blows instead, unless they have been guilty of certain enumerated crimes. Why astronomers should thus receive peculiar favor not conceded to other people does not appear. If a son, at a distance from home, enters into a marriage contract in ignorance of an engagement which his father may have made for him at home, he must give up his own choice, and marry the person chosen by his parents. An official may not marry the daughter of any one living under his jurisdiction. Marriage within certain degrees of consanguinity is not only strictly forbidden, but persons of the same surname who marry are liable to have the contract canceled and the wedding presents confiscated to the government. At first thought this provision may appear to work no practical hardship, but as there are only four hundred and eight surnames among the four hundred millions of the Chinese, the law is more likely to interfere with matrimonial engagements than in other lands, where no limit is fixed to family names.

One provision of the code might well be copied in the statutes of every people. When a marriage engagement is proposed, it must be made clear to the families of the bride and bridegroom, that neither of them is "infirm, diseased, or over or under age." Deception upon any of these points is severely punished.

With a system of laws on the whole so moderate and reasonable, and an ample arrangement of checks and precautions against injustice, it might be expected that wrong would seldom go unpunished and innocence never fail of recognition. Yet the practical workings of Chinese courts of law show that bribery, extortion, and cruel injustice are not merely possible, but easy and common under the most elaborate system that can be devised. There are no juries, and lawyers are unknown. Cases are decided not so much by direct reference to the law as by precedents. This practice has called into existence a class of unofficial hangers-on about the courts who are called "searchers." They have no recognized standing, have been denounced again and again by high officials, and their employment by magistrates forbidden by the Emperor; yet they continue to exist and to pursue their calling throughout the empire. It is their business, when any particular case is to come up for adjudication, to examine the records and find a similar or parallel case which may serve as a model or guide for the adjustment of that before the court. It is easily seen that with records running back almost to the beginning of time, any sort of a precedent may be found to suit the wishes of the " searcher ;" and it is just here that bribery, extortion, and blackmail are most commonly levied. No matter whether the accused be innocent or guilty, the searcher must be " seen" and his favorable report secured by a liberal fee. When it is added that these harpies have no other compensation than that secured from persons before the court, and that they are almost invariably wealthy, the whole story is told. It is believed that a Chinese magistrate seldom accepts a bribe directly. When he receives one, it is by a private commercial arrangement with these hangers-on of his court.

Great and dangerous latitude is given to Chinese magistrates as to the means which they may legally employ to extort the truth from parties to a case or from witnesses. An oath is rarely administered, and never relied upon. Perjury, as a crime, is unknown. The Chinese act upon the theory that, if a man will lie in any case, no oath will make him truthful. In fact, no Chinese judge expects either party or any witness to tell the exact truth. This is to be got at, first, by examining all parties separately, and by shrewd cross-questions in case the evidence is conflicting, as is invariably the case. If this fails, the persons whose stories fail to agree are confronted with each other, and each made to repeat his evidence in the other's presence, the judge carefully studying the countenance and general demeanor of each, and by these and other signs deciding which is telling the truth ; and they become very expert at this practice.

When these modes fail, the magistrate is allowed

to order the persons suspected of false testimony to be beaten in order to extort the truth. It is not uncommon for a judge to pause in the midst of his questions, and order the person under examination beaten across the mouth with a bamboo switch until the blood flows. Then, after a warning that worse will come if he persists in his untruths, the examination continues. They may also cause even a witness to kneel for hours upon chains, to be suspended by the thumbs, or to be confined for a long period with little or nothing to eat or drink. Other tortures still more severe and not authorized by law are on rare occasions employed.

Great importance is laid upon securing a confession from a person accused of crime. Tortures too horrible for description are sometimes made use of to accomplish this end, and often the prisoner confesses to a crime which he never committed, in order to secure a short respite from unendurable cruelty. I once saw three Chinese, who had been accused of theft, urged to confession in the following manner. Each man's arms were brought behind his back and tightly lashed together at the wrists. A rope was then fastened to this lashing, the other end thrown over the limb of a tree, and the men in this manner were hoisted from the ground and allowed to hang for three hours in a blazing sun. When let down, they were insensible. Their arms were dislocated at the shoulders, black, and frightfully swollen. Brought to consciousness, they renewed their denials of guilt, but on preparations being made for a renewal of the torture, they were as eager to confess as they had been to deny their guilt. It is needless to add that such tortures are strictly prohibited by law, or that when subordinate officials report cases to the higher tribunals, if measures like these have been resorted to to procure an admission of guilt, they invariably fail to report the important fact.

It must not, however, be inferred that such horrible scenes are the rule in Chinese trials. They are exceptional. The majority of magistrates are upright and humane, even if ignorant, narrow-minded, and superstitious. It is amusing and yet not surprising to find certain antiquated and absurd methods practiced by them, which are identical in both idea and form with those in use in the courts of Europe two centuries ago. In coroners' inquests and trials for murder this is strikingly true. A suspected murderer is brought into the presence of the victim and made to touch the body, when, if he is guilty, the wounds will bleed afresh. In inquests where poison is suspected as the cause of death, a silver needle is thrust into the body. If poison was administered, the needle on being withdrawn will have a greenish color. The bones are also examined in cases of suspected poison, and they are supposed to show the presence of the fatal drug by a similar change from their natural appearance.

The administration of justice in China, like the entire governmental system, is based upon the parental idea. The magistrate seldom forgets that he is theoretically the father of the people living under his jurisdiction; and it is not at all unusual for him to mingle the examination and cross-examination of witnesses or principals in any given case with exhortations and admonitions to tell the truth. He will cajole, entreat, threaten, and advise a recalcitrant person all in one breath, quote Confucius to him, ask him irrelevant questions, and assure him of his fatherly regard, and through it all watch him with the utmost keenness, ready to catch any word that may furnish a clew to what he is, through all this rigmarole, in search of—the truth.

It was once my fortune to sit on the bench with a Chinese magistrate in the trial of seven men accused of being the ringleaders in the attack of a mob upon an American citizen. The men were coal-miners, and had beaten the foreigner with small rope mats well saturated with coal-dust, which they wore as pads upon their shoulders in bringing lumps of coal out of the pit. The coal-dust made these mats as dangerous as sand-bags, and had they hit the American a single heavy blow upon the head, would have killed him. There was no possible doubt of the guilt of the persons. The attack was made at noon in the central square of the city, and a hundred witnesses could be brought to identify them. The examination was conducted much as follows. After asking the names of each of the accused, the magistrate, a venerable and pleasant-faced man of seventy years, turned to one of them and said, in a familiar way:

"You tell us all about it now. What did you beat the American for? Tell us the whole story."

"But I did not beat him, your Excellency," said

the man; "I wasn't there. Besides, I am a good man. A thousand times ten thousand it is true that I never touched him."

"Oh, yes! We know all about that," rejoined the official, returning to the charge. "Such a good Son of Han as you are wouldn't harm a baby; but, all the same, what made you do it? Don't you know that Confucius declares that all men within the four seas are brethren? Why should you wish to harm your brother? Of course we know you did not do it; were, in fact, in bed and asleep when the deed was done. At the same time we know that you did do it, and it will save us a lot of bother if you confess. Of course you did not mean any harm; we are sure of that. You wanted a little fun, and had heard some talk about the streets that if some one would only frighten the foreigner, or give him a drubbing, he would leave town and never return; and so you thought you would try it. Certainly you were not there, but you beat him just the same as though you were. Now, look at this gentleman on the bench here with me. He has come all the distance from Peking to attend to this business. He is a United States officer, and I shall punish you exactly as he desires. He has found out all about it, gave me your name, and asked me to have you arrested; but you can see by his face that he is good-natured. You tell us all about it, and he will let you off easily. Besides, he is in a hurry to get back to Peking, and has promised that if we finish this business to-day he will dine with me to-morrow. You would not put him to delay and inconvenience, now, would you? He knows all about it. Meet him half-way, now, and confess."

Thus the garrulous old man ran on for more than an hour, quizzing, bantering, and persuading the accused, who, whenever an opening gave him chance to be heard, reiterated his innocence, but in tones noticeably growing fainter and less positive. At last he said: "But I did not hit him as hard as some of the others did." Quick as a flash the magistrate retorted: "You did hit him, then? Come, now, tell us about it." And then the prisoner, with his head hanging down and with the air of a school-boy caught sticking pins into the master's chair, said: "Well, if I must, I must. Perhaps I did give him a shove."

"That is right," said the judge, "we knew you did; but it is always right to confess." Then turning to me, he asked: "What punishment shall I give this man?" I named what seemed a proper penalty, and sentence was at once given. The other prisoners admitted at once their share in the offense, and the remainder of the trial did not occupy ten minutes.

A member of the Prison Reform Society would, undoubtedly, be shocked beyond expression at what he might see in the best prison within the limits of the Chinese Empire. And they are loathsome, horrible dungeons, often the scenes of cruelty and barbarism too fearful for description; yet two important facts must be kept in mind regarding them. In the first place, any prison, in order to serve the purpose of its establishment, must be an object of terror to the lower and criminal classes in the country where it is located. Residence within its walls must mean actual suffering and hardship; and any person who is at all familiar with the manner in which the poorer classes of the Chinese live in their own homes, will at once realize the fact that a prison in that land must, indeed, be a horrible place if it is to have any restraining influence. The fact is, that if the worst prison in the United States were duplicated anywhere in the Chinese Empire, at least one half the population entitled to accommodations in it would hasten to commit such crimes as would entitle them to a cell, and would exercise anxious care that the offense should be of such a nature as to secure to them the privileges of a long residence in it.

In the second place, imprisonment is not a legal punishment for crime in China. Prisons are merely houses of detention for witnesses, persons accused of offense against the laws of the empire, and criminals under sentence, but awaiting the infliction of the prescribed penalty. No such thing is known in Chinese courts as a sentence to a term of imprisonment. This fact renders the horrors and infamous cruelties of these prisons more inexcusable, since they are perpetrated upon persons charged with no offense, such as witnesses and other persons accused but innocent; and there are few conceivable horrors that have failed to be realized in these houses of death. The native who wrote the Chinese word for "hell" upon the door of a Peking prison employed only a very moderate term of description.

There are five forms of punishment recognized

in Chinese law. These are flogging, wearing the "kang," branding, banishment, and death. Of these only the second needs a description. The kang, as prescribed in the penal code, is "a square frame of dry wood, three feet long, two feet nine inches wide, and weighing in ordinary cases thirty-three pounds." Its weight may be increased, in proportion to the gravity of the offense, up to one hundred and twenty-five pounds. It is made in two parts, which are hinged together at one side and provided with a lock at the other. In the centre is cut a circular opening the size of a person's neck. Its manner of use is apparent. It is opened, adjusted about the neck of the person condemned to wear it, and then closed and locked. A strip of paper is pasted on either side of the head of the wearer. One states his name, age, and place of residence; the other, his crime and the number of days he is to wear this unwholesome collar. It cannot be removed, night or day, during the prescribed term. The wearer cannot reach his mouth, and hence must be fed by others. He is daily led about the streets, and at night locked in prison. He cannot lie down, but must sleep in an upright position.

There are three forms of inflicting the death penalty. That considered least disgraceful is by strangulation; next is decapitation; last and most degrading is by slicing, in which the victim is slowly cut in pieces. This last is only inflicted as a punishment for high treason and for that gravest of all crimes according to the Chinese idea of the sacredness of the parental relation, for the crime of murder of parent or grandparent. Strangulation is performed by slipping a rope loosely about the victim's neck, a stick is thrust within it at the back of the head, and the executioner twists this until death ensues. Decapitation is effected by a heavy two-handed sword. The criminal is placed upon his knees, his hands being lashed together behind his back ; his head is drawn forward, and a single blow given upon the back of the neck severs the head from the body.

As Confucius taught that it was the first duty of every person to return his body to his ancestors as complete in all its members as when he received it from them, large sums of money are sometimes paid by the friends of decapitated criminals for the privilege of sewing the head upon the body before burial. While this privilege can be secured, it is always accompanied with one condition. The head must be reversed—that is, sewn on back side foremost. It may be said, in passing, that this doctrine of Confucius leads many Chinese to suffer death rather than to consent to the loss of any part of the body by a surgical operation.

A peculiar form of favor is sometimes shown to high officials, and especially to members of the imperial family, who may have been condemned to the death penalty. Suicide being considered less disgraceful than any form of death at the hands of the public executioner, the victim receives a handsome lacquer box wrapped in silk of the color sacred to the Emperor. Upon opening the box a white silken cord is found, neatly coiled, lying within. This is a silent but stern suggestion to the recipient to take his own life by means of the rope thus provided. If he fails to act upon the hint within twenty-four hours, the public executioner claims him.

The foreign observer in a Chinese court of law remarks, first, its total unlikeness to anything in foreign lands. The only person seated is the magistrate. Officers of the court and all spectators are required to stand. Prisoners and witnesses must be upon their hands and knees, and remain there so long as they are in the presence of the court. This rule sometimes gives rise to awkward and yet amusing controversies.

In the winter of 1873 two American residents of Peking became involved in a difficulty with a Chinese contractor, who, having secured in advance a considerable sum of money, refused to complete a building according to agreement. As a result of correspondence between the United States Legation and the Foreign Office, the matter was referred to a member of the latter body and myself for adjustment. The contractor and the two Americans having been summoned to appear before us, a grave question arose at once as to the position to be taken by these parties while in court. As the entire proceeding was informal, I proposed that they should come in and sit down. My Chinese colleague was horrified at the suggestion. He should require the Chinese to get upon his hands and knees, and as all parties manifestly ought to receive the same treatment, the Americans must assume the same attitude. Where was the dignity of the court, if suppliants could swagger into

its presence and be treated as its equals? He
would be laughed and ridiculed into retirement
if he allowed a Chinese to sit in court, and if
Americans were allowed that privilege he should
decline to go on with the case. I was so much
amused at the idea of requiring two free American
citizens, both my seniors, and one gray-headed,
and at the brilliant success I should achieve if I
made such a preposterous demand upon them,
that I found some difficulty in replying connectedly
to the argument of my Chinese associate. However, I managed to say that no such custom was
known in America, where the worst criminal was
only required to stand when addressed by his
judges; that what he insisted upon was by us
regarded as degrading, and could not be considered
for a moment.

After a long and heated discussion it was finally
agreed that each officer should follow the practice
in vogue in his own country—that is to say, he
should require the Chinese contractor to kneel,
and I should request my fellow-citizens to remain
standing while in our presence; and the case was
heard and satisfactorily adjusted upon that basis.

A similar but far more serious case arose at
Foochow in 1877. It became my duty, in con-
junction with the Chief Justice of the Supreme
Court of the province, to examine a large number
of Chinese witnesses in a case of bribery. Near
the close of the investigation it appeared important
to have the evidence of a Chinese subject, who
was an officer in the United States Consulate, and
held a letter of appointment from the Secretary of

State at Washington. In this peculiar position he was not amenable to Chinese law except by our consent, and could only be summoned by me. At the request of the Chief Justice I agreed to produce him, but with the express condition that he should be treated like an American witness. This was distinctly agreed to, and the next day this witness appeared.

As soon as he came into court the Chief Justice called out: "Get down upon your hands and knees."

"I beg your pardon," said I, "but this witness was not to be required to kneel."

"I don't care anything about that," replied the Chief Justice; "he is Chinese, and must obey Chinese law. Kneel down."

"You are violating a positive promise," said I; "the witness shall not kneel."

"Kneel down," said the Justice.

"Stand up," said I.

"Get down upon your knees," screamed the Justice.

"Leave the room," said I.

The frightened and bewildered witness obeyed me, and fairly ran from the room. Much sharp talk followed, the result of which was that the Chief Justice apologized, whereupon the witness was recalled and examined standing.

This case illustrated the extreme point to which injustice and brutality can go in a Chinese court of law. The only parties guilty of wrongdoing were a Chinese merchant and the interpreter to the United States Consulate. The former was not placed on trial at all. He had arranged matters to his own satisfaction with the Chinese authorities, and appeared in court as the friend and confidential adviser of the Chief Justice! The interpreter, though Chinese by birth, was a naturalized British subject, and hence equally free from all responsibility to either American or Chinese law. He was summarily discharged from office, but beyond that could not be touched.

The only sufferers were some thirty ignorant native fishermen, all innocent of any offense against the law, at least so far as the evidence showed. It was in August, the heat intense, and the city fairly reeking with cholera, yet these men had been thrown into a prison indescribable in its horrors, and beaten, tortured, and starved for months before they were brought into court. They all bore marks of fearful suffering, and of the thirty, only twenty-three lived to give evidence at the trial. One of these was brought into court like a log by four constables, who endeavored to prop him up upon his hands and knees; but he was so nearly dead that he fell over on his face, and was finally examined lying at full length upon the floor. He could speak only in a whisper, and a word or two at a time.

During the examination I noticed him feebly fumbling in the bosom of his tattered garment, and presently the end of a bit of folded paper showed itself between his fingers. An attendant of the Chief Justice sprang at once to seize it, but my attendant, to whom I had quietly spoken, was quicker, and secured it. The paper proved to be a petition to me for help and protection. It detailed a record of hideous torture, from the effects of which seven men had died, though no crime was proved or charged even against any one of them. But, so far as the Chinese parties in the case were concerned, I was absolutely powerless, and could only look on with disgust and horror at the fearful injustice disclosed. Any attempt at interference would have been resented, and would have reacted upon the poor wretches who appealed for help. It is but just to say that in many years of varied experience in Chinese courts, this was the only instance of outrageous brutality that came within my knowledge.

One ancient rule of Chinese court procedure, not now generally followed, is amusing, and yet contains more grains of wisdom than at first thought may appear. It provided that whenever two litigants appeared before a magistrate, he should, at the very outset, and prior to hearing any statement of the case at issue or examining either of the parties, order each, with absolute impartiality, "to be flogged with thirty blows of the small bamboo." The purpose was to warn them not to rush lightly into litigation, or trouble the magistrate without grave cause.

CHAPTER X.

OFFICIALS AND PEOPLE.

The relationship existing between the Chinese and their local authorities furnishes a most curious, interesting, and perplexing study. It presents many apparent and startling contradictions, and really exhibits a new and distinct phase of the national character. No man is more cautious, shrewd, and exact in his business affairs than the average Chinese merchant. He knows his own, and exacts it down to the last fraction. He will argue and quarrel with a business associate for half a day over the hundredth part of a cent, and year after year readily and cheerfully pay taxes in a dozen different forms to the collector, knowing well that in each item the amount which he pays is very considerably larger than the law demands. He will submit to other forms of official injustice without protest or murmur, and come to blows with a neighbor or lifelong friend over some trivial breach of etiquette which, in his opinion, affects his dignity or honor. I have known two brothers to quarrel bitterly because one called the other by his given name instead of addressing him as " Venerable Elder Brother," and each of them had been

the victim of official cruelty and injustice without thought of complaint.

This peculiarity cannot be explained by the assumption that the people are either ignorant of or indifferent to their rights. Nor are they stolid and heedless, lacking nerves, as some have asserted. Nor, again, is it generally fear of the authorities, dread of punishment, which leads them to submit. They speak of the Emperor, it is true, with bated breath; but no such reserve affects their ideas or their speech in regard to the local authorities. They are very democratic in their criticisms of them, realize that they all are of the people, like themselves, and are quite free with their praise or censure. They are very fond of slang names, and generally dub each official by such as in their opinion fits some peculiarity of speech, appearance, or conduct. Even the very highest officials are not exempt from these pet names. Prince Kung is indifferently called by the people of Peking "Head Clerk Number 6," because he was at the head of the government and the sixth son of a former Emperor, or "Devil Number 6," because he was supposed to be friendly toward foreigners, for whom "Devil" is the ordinary slang name. A certain member of the Cabinet was practically never spoken of by his proper name or title, but invariably by the Chinese name for the measuring-worm, with which every one is familiar; and on one occasion a member of the Privy Council spoke to me of the Emperor as "our Boss."

With all his superstitious notions, fads, and fancies, the Chinese is essentially a practical man of business. He indulges little in sentiment. He is more of a philosopher than an enthusiast, and seldom enters upon a path to which the end is invisible. This element in his character has, undoubtedly, much to do with his quiet submission to real or fancied injustice. He will not revolt against any moderate extortion until fully convinced that such action will pay. If, in his judgment, it will cost him more to secure his rights than the commercial value of those rights, it is idle to appeal to him. He will not move. He knows by experience or observation the worry, expense, and possible danger of active opposition to the local authorities, and prefers to bear the ills that he sees rather than fly to those he knows not.

Another important factor in the question needs notice. The nominal salaries of Chinese officials is notoriously inadequate. In the majority of cases the sum specified as compensation is not enough to provide the underlings, clerks, and other subordinates which the magistrate is not only obliged to have, but also to pay. When we bear in mind that a distinguished Secretary of State at Washington paid his entire official salary to his butler, and remember that in few or none of our diplomatic establishments in Europe is the salary of a Secretary of Legation sufficient to pay the rent of a decent house in a decent locality, we can appreciate the difficulties under which Chinese officials labor in this regard. The government so far recognizes this fact as to make to each official an allowance from the "anti-extortion fund." This allowance is, in some instances, as much in amount as twenty

THE GREAT WALL.

or twenty-five times the salary, and still both combined are not sufficient to support the official with a decent show of dignity.

This fact is universally known and recognized. From it has sprung the idea commonly accepted, that every official has a right to receive a fair amount of extra compensation for every service rendered to the people. If they trouble him with legal cases, he has a right to expect pay for it. If he collects the taxes, it is only fair that he should receive and reserve a commission for himself. His salary is a merely nominal affair. He looks to the residents within his jurisdiction for his support. The validity of such a claim is admitted in every district in the empire, and no complaint is ever made against it unless the sum demanded is exorbitant in amount, or exacted for services not properly rendered. To a Western mind the evils of such a system are far too plain to need comment or explanation; yet a Chinese would fail to see any approach to bribery or corruption in it, and stoutly defend the practice as only reasonable and business-like.

A modification of this plan is in force between officials of various grades, from the lowest even to those about the very presence of the Emperor. A titled Chinese, who represented his government for many years with distinguished ability abroad, once told me that on the occasion of his first call in Peking upon one of the members of the imperial family, his attendant carried a present of one hundred ounces of silver, which was delivered to the officer on duty at the door where the call was made, and that on each subsequent visit half that sum was taken. He added that there was a regular scale of "presents," graded according to the rank of the visitor upon him of princely blood, and that what he had taken was the amount fixed for persons of his rank. Another official, upon his return from a post of duty, applied to the Court Chamberlain for the customary audience with the Emperor, and was informed that the usual present for persons of his rank was five thousand ounces of silver. He demurred at the amount, and offered one half. This being refused, he withdrew his request for audience, although by this course, as he well knew, further official employment was rendered impossible. Being a strictly honest servant of the State—and there are many such in China—he had not and could not procure so large a sum. A leading jeweler of Peking, on one occasion, showed me a hundred satin-lined and richly lacquered trays, each divided into ten compartments, each compartment fitted to receive a block of silver bullion weighing ten ounces. They were being prepared and were to be filled upon the order of a certain high official, who proposed to send a present of ten thousand ounces of silver in this elegant form to one of the princes.

One phase of this system of giving and receiving gifts is not without a certain redeeming feature. It has a practical value in enforcing the maintenance of peace and order. Under Chinese law there is no provision for the infliction of a fine in punishment for any class of offenses, though there are certain lesser penalties which the law allows to be commuted by payment of a specified sum ; and there is a large number of cases which are quietly condoned upon receipt of an amount of money generally in close approximation to the ability of the offender to pay. Probably none of this money finds its way into the public treasury, though cases have been known in which it was expended upon some much-needed public improvement ; but there is a generally recognized class of fines or money penalties levied upon subordinate officials by their superiors for failure or neglect of duty, in case of any complaints being made against them, and, in general, for any bother or trouble to those above them for which they are responsible.

Whatever may be said of the abstract honesty of such a system, it cannot be doubted that the direct result is to make those who are liable to its penalties both vigilant in the maintenance of order and cautious in their exactions from the people. If a district magistrate understands—and he does—that any complaint of extortion made against him will be at once followed by a demand, from the governor of the province, that he "divide" with him, he will be less shrewd than the average Chinese if he fails to guide his course by the plain reasoning that it is better to exact two thirds of a given sum and retain it all, than to collect the whole and be obliged to share half or more of it with those above him. In a similar way, any remissness in official duty sufficiently grave to provoke complaint is certain to be expensive to the offending official, even in cases where the complaint is really trivial or not well founded. A single illustration will show what is meant. I once had occasion to report a case of theft to the police magistrate near the United States Legation in Peking. The burglar had entered the rooms of the Chinese copyist employed in the Legation, and stolen a few silver ornaments worth not more than twelve or fifteen dollars. Liberal promises were made by the magistrate, but nothing was accomplished, and the affair passed out of sight. Three months later a thief entered my own house, and escaped with property of more value. The same magistrate was sent for, and under the pressure of threats of being reported to the military governor of the city, he secured the thief and every stolen article within twenty hours of the robbery. Some weeks later the magistrate asked for an interview, and upon being admitted, placed upon my desk the silver ornaments stolen from the copyist, not one being missing. I expressed my surprise and gratification, whereupon the following conversation took place :

"They have made me a great deal of trouble and cost me much money. If you had only warned me before you complained to the General of the Nine Gates (the military governor), I would have recovered them for you and saved the expense."

"But I made no complaint to the governor about this case."

"You must have done so, since he knew all about it."

"No. I never laid a complaint against you before him about this or any other case. I warned you that I would do so if you did not act promptly in securing the thief who entered my own house ; but your course was so satisfactory in that affair, and the value of these articles so trivial, that I decided not to press the matter ; and, in fact, had forgotten all about it."

"But did you say nothing to the General of the Nine Gates about this theft ?"

"Only indirectly. Of course I was obliged to see him a number of times regarding the punishment of the other thief whom you arrested. In the course of conversation I praised you for your prompt and satisfactory course, which, to be entirely frank, I told him was surprising as well as agreeable, since in an earlier but unimportant case, which I had referred to you, you had promised much and done nothing."

"That makes it all clear. He ordered me to appear before him, told me how pleased you were with my action, then forced me to tell him all about the first case, fined me one thousand ounces of silver, and warned me that if within a month I failed to secure this property and deliver it to you, he would fine me another equal amount and remove me from office. You need never complain again. No thief will disturb your Legation in future." And none did.

It may appear surprising, in view of what has preceded, that few nations have such a complete civil service as China, or one in which the checks and guards against injustice, oppression, and every form of maladministration have been so carefully, and with such apparent wisdom, wrought out. Yet such is the case. The regulations calculated to secure the people against official wrongdoing are elaborate, exhaustive, and minute in detail. Faithfully enforced under intelligent popular pressure—and any civil service is worthless without that—they would produce an ideal public service. Mention has already been made of the censorate, that body of independent watchdogs of the public welfare, whose eyes are supposed to be fastened in close scrutiny upon every official, no matter what his rank in the empire, and through whom the meanest subject may carry his wrongs, free of fear or expense, to the Emperor in person.

Some of the regulations governing appointments to office, and the conduct of those appointed, are worthy of recital, both as showing practical wisdom, and also the evils against which the central government has found it necessary to guard. No officer can occupy a post within the province where he was born. He cannot employ any relatives in any position, however menial. He cannot take a wife or a concubine from among the people over whom he has authority. No two persons related as closely as second cousins can hold office within the same province. Hardly a year passes without transfers being made under this rule. The foregoing are manifestly intended as guards against favoritism or injustice growing out of family influence. Another regulation to which the Chinese attach great importance limits the retention of any post to three years. At the termination of that period the officer is removed to some other point, and, theoretically at least, is given a more or less desirable position, as his record may warrant. On rare occasions, and in response to popular demand, he is given a second term at the same post, but, on the whole, the rule of change is faithfully enforced. The manifest intent of this provision is to preclude the formation of either such strong personal friendships or corrupt combinations as would affect the even-handed administration of affairs.

Much has been written, and many amusing, though perhaps apocryphal stories told regarding the sale of offices in China, and the absurd and grotesque conduct of those who have thus secured position and power. The author is convinced that these statements are not borne out by the facts, but are the natural result of the confusion of two distinct and different honors, each of which is eagerly sought after by the people. Undoubtedly the right to use an official title and to wear the button which represents it upon the hat has been, in times of special stress, sold to a very large extent. Such honors are also not infrequently granted by the Emperor to public-spirited individuals who have contributed funds to build bridges, repair roads or dykes, or rendered conspicuous service in other directions. Such honors carry with them certain legally defined special privileges, but they never confer the right to hold office. The author has known many Chinese who had thus bought or earned official title, but he has never met one who was an office-holder, nor, as the result of an inquiry of considerable length, has he found a Chinese who knew or had heard of any official above the rank of village constable who had secured a position by such means. Titular honors and dignities can be purchased, but the road to office lies exclusively through the educational examinations, controlled and conducted by the government. It

CHINESE BEGGAR.

would not be equally safe to deny that money has smoothed the path to promotion when once those examinations have been successfully passed.

Public opinion plays an essential part in the control of the conduct of Chinese officials. Any magistrate who ignores it, or outrages the feelings of the people, is certain, sooner or later, to come to grief. He has three duties to perform. He must preserve peace and order, collect and remit the amount of taxes apportioned to his district, and see to it that no complaints are made against him. Within these three points he is practically left untrammeled. His district is farmed out to him, and few questions are asked concerning his methods, so long as questions are not provoked by charges of maladministration coming from those whom he governs. The people, upon their part, have a far more intelligent conception of what the proper duties and authority of an official are than might be expected. As has been stated, they allow him a very liberal latitude beyond the strict letter of the law, but are quick to show their displeasure when he goes too far; and a record of an unpopular administration has a very damaging effect upon a local magistrate when, at the close of the prescribed three years' term of service at one post, the question of his transfer arises. In this way self-interest serves as a valuable check to what the Chinese would regard as unreasonable excess of authority.

Scattered throughout all parts of the empire is a class of men known among foreigners as "the literati." They are the educated men of the communities where they reside. They have completed the necessary course of study, and have passed one or more of the government examinations which form the preliminary test to office-holding. As near as any correspondences can be said to exist between things Oriental and our Western ways, they may be compared to college-bred men among us who are not in official life. There is this essential difference, however. All of these Oriental graduates pursued their course of study with a direct view to office-holding as a lifelong career. All are possible office-holders, and a majority are hopeful and expectant of that distinction.

These are the influential men in every community, as would be expected. They have certain legal privileges and immunities which no power less exalted than the governor of a province can curtail or remove. In a measure they are, therefore, independent of the local authority. As they consider it undignified to engage in labor or trade, nothing but the sharp necessity of actual suffering will drive them to work; hence, as a rule, they have abundant leisure in which to watch those into whose shoes they hope some day to step. Since they esteem themselves as belonging to the ruling class, they are generally moderate in their criticisms of those in office; but they mould, control, and guide public opinion. They are invariably the arbitrators in the settlement of disputes among the people, and in all questions at issue between the people and their magistrates. They constitute a sort of unofficial extra legal jury, always in session. The central government manages to keep in touch with them through the censorate, and, as a rule, shows great deference to their opinions, which it recognizes as the exponent of the popular will.

The controlling, moderating influence which such a body of men must exercise upon an official inclined either to cruelty or greed must be readily seen. They belong to his class in society, many of them hope at some time to occupy a position similar to his; hence they are inclined to exercise charity in their judgment of his acts. Upon the other hand, their families, relatives, and friends are among those who must suffer from his wrongdoing, and they cannot be silent to their appeals. Upon his part, the magistrate needs the moral support of this class in aid of his authority, and thus they become a sort of balance-wheel or regulator in every district in China.

As between officials and people, it may be readily admitted that the intervention of the literati is commonly in the interests of good government, and beneficial; but they are credited with the use of their power in other directions, in which it has worked great injury to the State, cost it large sums in the way of indemnities, and, more than once, brought it to the verge of war. The Chinese literati arrogate to themselves the conservatism of public morals and the preservation of the ancient traditions and policy. Each of their number considers himself as a practical reincarnation of Confucius, and as a depository of the wisdom and infallibility of that sage. What he knew, they know; and anything beyond the bounds of their learning is either inherently vicious or worthless. Hence, opposition to progress centres itself in them. They are bigoted and fanatical. They are accused, on apparently good grounds, with stirring up the people against foreigners and of inciting many of the outbreaks of mob violence, particularly those in which missionaries have been the objects of attack. While they pride themselves upon their conservative influence and power as a body, they, in fact, constitute a most serious menace to the prosperity and well-being of the nation.

The Chinese people have some peculiar methods of exhibiting their approval of the conduct of a magistrate. A red silk umbrella, not to be carried over the head, but by an attendant in advance of the owner, is a sign of high official state. Such an umbrella, provided by popular subscription and inscribed with a complimentary phrase or two and the names of the donors, is sometimes presented with great parade to a magistrate who has earned the approval of his people. A tablet or a silken scroll, similarly inscribed, is also given as a mark of appreciation. In June, 1870, the prefectural magistrate at Tientsin was presented with such an umbrella, and also a tablet. The former bore the inscription, "An umbrella of ten thousand names," by which was meant that it was the expression of the good-will of the entire city. The tablet was inscribed, "A Buddha sprung from ten thousand families." In this delicate way the recipient was complimented as being the Buddha, the protector of the people.

These particular gifts illustrate the dangerous power exercised by the literati, and to which reference has just been made. They were, beyond a doubt, presented to the official named by the literati as a reward for conduct on his part which

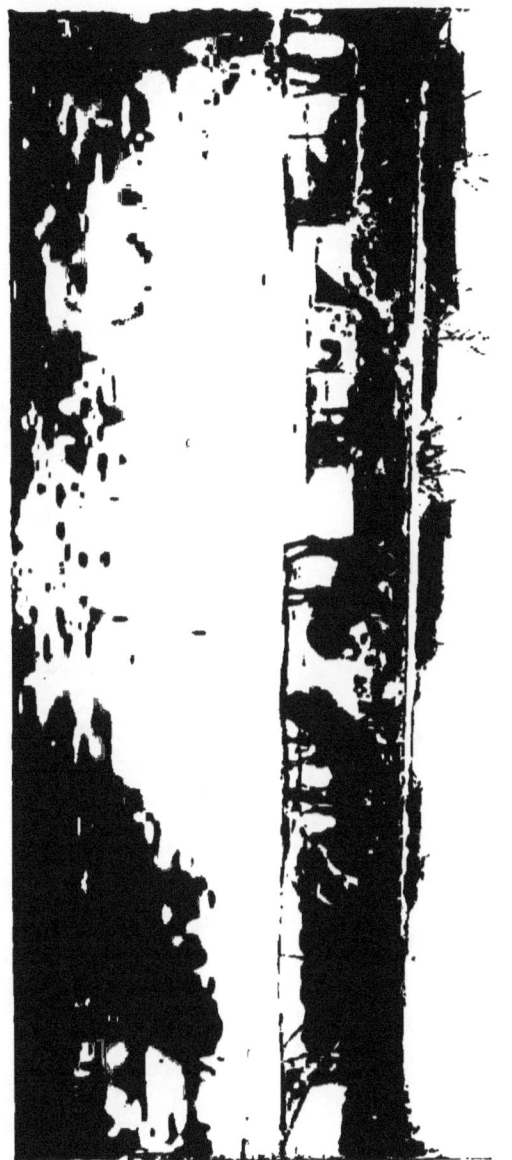
MONGOL WINTER ENCAMPMENT.

directly caused the horrible massacre at Tientsin, and which occurred only three days after the presentation was made. In this instance it may properly be said that the action of the literati and their influence with the people led directly to this appalling result. It cost the lives of twenty-three foreigners, most of whom were ladies, put to death in a manner far too fearful to be described. The magistrate paid for his umbrella and tablet by hard labor for life as a prison convict beyond the Amoor River. Twenty natives were beheaded, a large number were punished in other ways, and the Chinese Government further atoned for the misconduct of its officials by an indemnity of nearly $500,000 in gold, and a special mission of apology to France.

As a traveler enters the gate of any Chinese city he is liable to see suspended within the archway several pairs of boots, in various stages of preservation. These indicate another mode, and one quite unique, by which the people indicate their approval of the course taken by their magistrates. When a popular official is about to lay down the seal of office at the conclusion of his term of service, he is waited upon by a deputation of leading residents, who, with many flowery words of compliment and praise, gravely request him to donate to the city a pair of his official boots. The request is esteemed an honor, and is always granted. They are taken in solemn procession, with music and much parade, to the city gate and there suspended, where they remain until they decay and drop to pieces.

That the people can and do successfully resist injustice and extortion upon the part of their officials is being constantly shown. An incident within my own knowledge which illustrates this fact, shows their peculiar methods, and exhibits the forbearance and moderation with which they made use of their victory, may well close this chapter.

The land tax is fixed by imperial decree—that is, by law—at a certain number of decimal parts of an ounce of silver on each Chinese acre. As individual land-holdings are small, and the amount of the tax in each case insignificant, it is almost invariably paid in copper cash. The equivalent of an ounce of silver in cash varies a few pieces from day to day, but it stands substantially at two thousand pieces of cash per ounce. This fluctuation in the value of silver, slight as it is, furnishes the magistrate with an opportunity, of which he rarely fails to take advantage, to exact more cash in payment of the land tax than the market value of the bullion will warrant. In a certain district city less than a hundred miles from Peking the magistrates had for many years collected this tax in cash at the rate of four thousand pieces for an ounce of silver —a profit to themselves of nearly one hundred per cent. This was paid willingly and without any question. As has been pointed out, the people realized the fact that the officials must live. A new incumbent increased the rate to five thousand pieces, and this was quietly paid. Misunderstanding the temper of his constituency, after a few months he raised the rate of exchange to six thousand. Then they grumbled, but they paid. A further increase to seven thousand provoked talk of organized opposition, but nothing practical resulted from it. Before the first half of his term of office had expired he raised the rate again, demanding eight thousand cash for an ounce of silver, or about four times the legitimate amount.

This brought matters to a crisis. A mass-meeting was held, at which it was decided to present a petition to the Emperor, through the censorate, setting forth their grievances and asking for the immediate disgrace of the rapacious magistrate. Being within easy reach of Peking, it was decided at the meeting to send a deputation thither with their memorial and complaint, in order to hasten the redress of their wrongs. The documents were accordingly prepared and a committee of three influential literati carried them to the capital, and there presented them to the Supreme Court of the censorate.

Now the regulations prescribing the form, shape, and style in which all classes of official documents must be prepared in China are exceedingly rigorous and minute in detail. They must be written upon a peculiar quality of paper, of a particular shade of color. Certain characters must be elevated just so many points and no more above their fellows. The document must be folded to exactly so many inches in width, endorsed, sealed, enveloped, and superscribed in absolute conformity to a specified plan.

Unfortunately for the deputation, their memorial failed in one or two unimportant details of being in exact conformity to regulations. It was returned to them unread, they were each favored with fifty blows of the bamboo, and fined a small sum for contempt of court. They returned home sore and crestfallen, and the local magistrate, in too great haste as the event proved, signalized his victory by increasing the official rate of exchange to nine thousand pieces of cash for an ounce of silver.

He knew little of Chinese human nature. Another meeting was at once called, papers were more carefully drawn up, to which another count in the indictment of the magistrate was added, and another deputation bore them to the capital. This time they were successful. The offending official was degraded, stripped of his rank, and forbidden to apply for future official employment; and a magistrate having an exceptionally good record was sent to them. He at once, upon assuming office, called a meeting of the people, at which the question of a fair official rate of exchange between silver and cash was fully and freely discussed, and it was agreed with entire unanimity that five thousand cash should be the rate. A granite slab was prepared, upon which was cut the statement that at a meeting held that day it was agreed and understood between the magistrate and people that, for all future time, taxes might be paid in cash at the fixed rate of five thousand per ounce of silver; and this memorial and evidence of the agreement was formally set up in the great square at the centre of the town.

CHAPTER XI.

EDUCATION AND LITERATURE.

"NIEN shu, tso kuan" is a phrase heard from the lips of every parent and every male child in the Chinese Empire. It means "secure an education and become an official," and indicates, what has already been said, that the object of all study in China and the supreme ambition is official life. Every boy who goes to school goes with this purpose, at least when he is old enough to have any thought about the matter, and all parents who seek education for their sons do it with this hope and desire in mind.

The history of the nation justifies this ambition. For many centuries the practical government has been in the hands of those who have sprung from the common people, and who, starting from the general level, have, by means of an education, climbed step by step up the ladder of influence and honor, until they stood at the very top. While we have our list of poor boys who have become great men, such as Lincoln, Grant, Garfield, and others, they have a similar list vastly longer, as their country is older than ours. There is a countless number of school-boys in China to-day who are inspired and stimulated by these names, and by the possibilities which such careers open to them. Their examples are as well known and as widely honored as are ours. They all know that only a few years since a Chinese Prime Minister died who was a poor farmer's son, was himself poor all his life, yet of whom the Emperor said in a decree announcing his death: "He truly was my right arm and strong heart." And they all know, too, that the Emperor sent a prince of the blood, with ten of his own body-guard, to watch by the coffin of the deceased statesman so long as it remained in Peking, and directed the viceroy of the province of which the dead man was a native to attend the burial in person, in order to show the respect and honor in which he was held.

Those who have a vague idea that China is a heathen country of vast population, entirely given up to the practice of cruel and debasing superstitions, will find in Chinese books much to enlarge and modify their opinion of that empire. They will be astonished at the amount of sound instruction, pure morality, and wise, judicious counsel of a type so elevated that it well might be taught to Western children, as, indeed, it is, which they will find in the books prepared for use in the schools of China. A distinguished commentator upon the writings of Confucius prepared a volume adapted to primary instruction some seven hundred and seventy-five years ago, which is still used, unrevised and unchanged, in every school-room in the land. In the introduction a plan of life, so to speak, is marked out. The writer says that, when they are able to talk, "boys should be instructed to answer in a quick, bold tone, and girls in a slow and gentle voice." What follows refers to boys only. "At seven they should be taught to count and name the cardinal points, but should not be allowed to sit upon the same mat nor eat at the same table with their elders. At eight they must be taught to wait for their superiors, and prefer others to themselves. At ten they must be sent abroad to private tutors, and there remain day and night, studying writing and arithmetic, wearing plain apparel, learning to demean themselves in a manner becoming their age, and acting with sincerity of purpose. At thirteen they must attend to music and poetry, at fifteen they must practice archery and horsemanship. At the age of twenty they are to be admitted to the rank of manhood in due form, learn additional rules of propriety, be faithful in the performance of filial and fraternal duties, but must not affect to teach others, though possessed of extensive knowledge. At thirty they may marry and commence the conduct of business. At forty they may enter the service of the State ; at fifty be promoted to the rank of ministers, and at seventy they must retire from public life."

Other advice given in this text-book is as follows : " Let children always be taught to speak the simple truth, to stand erect and in their proper places, and listen with respectful attention." " The way to become a student is, with gentleness and self-abasement, to receive implicitly every word the master utters. The pupil, when he sees virtuous people, must follow them ; when he hears wise maxims, conform to them." "He must keep his clothes in order." "Every morning he must learn something new, and rehearse the same every evening." It hardly appears credible that a volume containing such wise advice and of so true a tone could have been in use as a text-book in the schools of China three and a half centuries before Columbus discovered America; yet such is the fact.

Another volume of equally high standard and of general use is called "The Complete Collection of Family Jewels." It contains a careful detail of the course to be pursued by all who would be thorough students. The keynote of the work is found in the sentence: "Better little and fine than much and coarse." The beginner is advised to form a fixed resolution to press forward in his studies, setting his mark as high as possible, and understanding everything as he goes along. The author also recommends all persons to have two or three good volumes lying upon their tables, which they can take up at odd moments, and to keep commonplace books, in which they can write down sentences worthy of being remembered. And a Chinese proverb, more ancient even than these books, yet everywhere quoted, declares that "three days without study renders a man's conversation insipid." One ceases to wonder at the permanence of Chinese institutions when he finds their educational system resting upon so high a level.

Sounder counsels and wiser maxims than these can be found in no country or age. Yet it must not be inferred that the Chinese course of study is,

as a whole or in part, so wisely chosen as these extracts might be supposed to indicate. Dr. S. Wells Williams has expressed the opinion in his work, " The Middle Kingdom," " That the great end of education among the ancient Chinese was not so much to fill the head with knowledge, as to discipline the heart and purify the affections." This may be true. If so, the end of education among the modern Chinese must be held to be the same, since the course of study has undergone no change for nearly a thousand years. But admiration for the wise moral sayings and good counsel is soon changed to utter astonishment when the course of study prescribed by government as competent to prepare men to fill the highest offices in the land is examined. It contains a sufficient amount of sound morality, as has been seen. Aside from that there is considerable superstitious teaching, many political maxims of more or less doubtful utility, bits of Chinese history and tradition, a smattering of local geography, and nothing else. Of these the history, whether exact or traditional, and the scraps of geography, are learned incidentally. They are not taught as distinct studies. Their accuracy, and hence their value, may be justly measured by the fact that they are found in the Confucian classics, which were written several hundred years before Christ.

Leaving out of sight the moral instruction, whose merits have been fully admitted, and taking the most favorable view possible of the Chinese system of education, it can only claim to accomplish the following results. It teaches reading and writing, versification, composition and style, and develops the memory to a marvelous extent. No people in the world have such mnemonic power as the Chinese.

The course of study is easily described. When the boy enters school, at five or six years of age, a book called the "Three-Character Classic" is given him. It is in rhyme—a sort of doggerel—and is made up of moral sayings and stories calculated to illustrate their excellence, by which he is taught to honor his father and mother, worship his ancestors, fear the Emperor, avoid bad company, attend to his books, and to practice other similar virtues. He is expected to commit this volume to memory—it is small—to learn the meaning and pronunciation of each character, and to write each correctly. When this task is completed he is given the "Book of the Hundred Family Names." This is also in rhyme, and is utterly devoid of sense, being nothing other than a list of the allowable surnames in the Chinese Empire. He must also commit this to memory, and learn to pronounce and write each character in it. This is followed by the "Lesser Instruction Book," or "The Complete Collection of Family Jewels," from both of which quotations have been made. These mastered in the same thorough manner as those which precede them, then comes the great and crowning task of student life. The nine volumes of the Confucian classics are spread before the pupil. These must be treated as were the others, memorized, and each character identified and written.

Exercises in versification and in composition are

given in connection with the study of Confucius. Some fine poetry has been written in China ; and it is only fair to say that many of her scholars are perfect masters of style. The language is concise, flexible, capable of expressing delicate shades of thought, and hence favors a high degree of attainment in this direction. I have seen and translated an official communication written by a noted Chinese scholar, the English version of which covered nearly a hundred pages, and, in the whole of the original text, not a single character could have been withdrawn or changed without affecting the sense.

The Confucian writings have already been sufficiently described. They contain a large amount of unimportant and valueless trash ; and it must also be said that they contain a great deal more which no man of modern times, be he Chinese or foreign, can in the least understand or explain. Those parts may have been the supremest wisdom when written, but in the many centuries since, whether from the entire change in the meaning of the characters, or in the use of words, or from some other unknown cause, no idea of any sort can be gained from them to-day. They are simply unsolved riddles, unguessable conundrums. I quote one sentence of this sort—an easy one—taken at random from the volume known as "The Book of Changes" : "The Great Man, assuming the appearance of the Tiger, refers to his luminous excellence." What can be made from such sheer nonsense as this ? Yet it is as good as, or possibly better than a large percentage of the contents of those nine sacred books, every character of which must be memorized and explained in some way by the student; and this completes the Chinese system of education.

Schools are found in every city, village, and hamlet in the empire. The public sentiment in favor of education is universal, and it is a reproach to any parents, however poor, if they neglect to send their sons to school. These are supported, not by the government, but by subscription or tuition fees, and the master, who must always have passed the official examinations, receives but small compensation, running from less than $75 a year in small villages to $150 a year in the larger towns and cities. Private tutors, who make a specialty of cramming young men for the examinations, and have a reputation for success in such work, often receive large sums.

The fittings of the school-rooms are primitive and meagre in the extreme. A square table, on which is placed a tablet of Confucius, and a chair beside it for the teacher, are the most important articles of furniture. Beside these there is a smaller table and a bench, such as would be called a carpenter's horse, for each pupil. These complete the furniture of the room. Each scholar has, besides his book, a few sheets of paper, an inkstone and stick of India ink (so called because it is made in China), a cup containing a little water with which to mix his ink, and a camel's-hair brush (so called because it is never made of camel's-hair). These complete his outfit. The master is commonly provided with a bamboo rod and an enormous pair of spectacles, the first as corrective medicine, with which boys in all lands are familiar, and the second as emblems of and aids to the essential dignity of his position.

The child makes his first appearance at school at the age of five or six, sometimes even younger, and attends nine hours a day, seven days in the week, until he has completed the course of study already described. This is generally accomplished by the time he is eighteen years old. Upon entering and leaving the room he must always make his obeisance to the tablet of Confucius and to the master. He is given a lesson in writing each day, and a portion of the book to commit to memory. He accomplishes this latter task by shouting it out, character by character, over and over again, at the top of his voice. If he is quiet, the bamboo rod is called into use. A thoroughly studious Chinese boy will almost raise the roof with the power of his lungs, and a well-ordered school-room makes itself known to a great distance. A factory or boiler-shop is quiet as a churchyard compared with it.

The instruction is entirely individual. Each pupil pursues his own studies, makes his own progress, quite independent of every other. When any one has learned the assigned task, he marches up to the master, hands him the book, then turns about and, with his back to the teacher and his hands folded behind him, recites his task. From this peculiar attitude is derived the Chinese idiomatic phrase, equivalent to the English word recitation, which means, literally translated, "to back the book."

There is no lack of evidence to demonstrate the fact that the Chinese, as a nation, possess a high average of intellectual ability. Their writings prove this; and a considerable number of recent tests show that they have no occasion to fear the results of direct competition, as students, with the young men and women in Western schools. A Chinese boy, who was given preliminary instruction in mission schools at Macao and Hongkong, and afterward sent to this country by the charity of the missionaries to complete his education, took the first prize in English composition at Yale College years ago. More recently a Chinese beggar girl, literally fished from a gutter in Peking one December night, where she had been thrown by her mother, and who had been sent to this country to complete her studies, graduated with first honors at one of our best female colleges. The Chinese boys sent to this country by their government for education according to the Western, or modern idea, furnish a striking proof of the high average of intellectual ability possessed by their race. These students were one hundred and twenty in number, and were sent here at the average age of eleven. All could read and write, but none of them knew any English, and not a half dozen had spent a day in any other than the ordinary Chinese school, already described. None of them were the sons of dukes and princes, as the American girls fondly imagined. They all came from middle-class families, reckoning from the native standpoint—that is, from families the head of which had an income of from $200 to $500 a year. Hardly a single case of either persistent misconduct or mental inability developed in the entire number. They mastered English, the third most difficult language in the world, with astonishing rapidity. They took hold of an entirely unfamiliar course of study with remarkable aptitude, and throughout the entire course, in primary, academic, collegiate, and technical schools held rank among the upper half of the students in their classes. Their deportment was simply unexceptionable. The author spent twenty-five days with fifty-one of these students upon crowded steamships crossing the Pacific, and he believes it impossible that the same number of American boys and young men from the same schools which these had attended could have been kept together so long and under circumstances so disagreeable, and shown such unqualified right to be regarded as gentlemen. They were under no surveillance, had no tutor or person of any authority in their company. Each was absolutely his own master. The president of one of the largest of American universities recently informed the author that five Chinese students— three boys and two girls—had been examined for admission into the collegiate department of the institution under his charge. None of them had had any preliminary education in this country, but had fitted for college in Chinese mission schools. Among several hundred candidates for admission, the Chinese boys took the highest percentage in Latin, and the girls in mathematics.

 Much has been written and many estimates made regarding the average of illiteracy in China. All such estimates are purely conjectural, and hence worthless. There are no data available upon which to base reliable calculations. It can only be said in a general way that the proportion of persons who can read and write varies greatly in different sections of the country. As might be expected, education is far more general in large towns and cities than in rural and remote districts. There is only one fact bearing upon this question which is fixed and certain. Female education is unknown. There are, practically, no schools for girls in the empire, excepting the mere handful supported and controlled by foreign missionaries. Hence, in any estimate of illiteracy, the entire female population, or fifty per cent of the whole, may at once be placed among the absolutely uneducated.

The government exercises no control or superintendence over the schools. It cannot be determined that the course of study was originally fixed by the authorities, as, if such was the case, it was done so long ago that the official record of the fact is lost in the obscurity of ages. All that can be asserted is that an Emperor of the Tang Dynasty, some nineteen hundred years ago, inaugurated the present plan of preparing and selecting officials by means of study and literary examinations. The system has not been essentially modified since. Like nearly all things else Chinese, it appears to have sprung into full form at once, and to have known neither growth nor decay.

There are certain classes of persons in the empire who, while not debarred from attending school, are forbidden, with their descendants to the fourth generation, from competing at the examinations, and, as a consequence, are incapable of holding office. These are persons convicted of crime against the State, theatrical performers and prostitutes, lictors, or persons who inflict punishment for crime, undertakers, barbers, table waiters, and body servants. A serious punishment is inflicted upon any person not more than four generations removed from either of these interdicted classes, who may have the temerity to enter his name upon the lists of candidates at any examination.

While some of these discriminations may seem plausible, even though unjust, others must strike the reader as utterly absurd and amusing. Thus a cook or any of his descendants may take a degree, and the path to the highest civil honors in the State lies broad and open before him; but that path is closed and barred to him who places the food, prepared by the cook, upon the table, and to his children down to the fourth generation. The artist who dresses and decorates the head, with his posterity, is placed under the ban. The gentleman who attends to the feet—the chiropodist—and his offspring are more fortunate, and may rise to any height of power and influence. Grotesque as these discriminations may appear, the Chinese, who seldom lack a reason for anything, have one here which is entirely satisfactory to them, however it may appear to Western minds. They insist that the butler and valet pursue menial callings, since each must stand in the presence of his master and in the performance of his duties. The cook is not thus degraded. Again, they maintain that since a barber must stand and his customer sit while the former plies the razor or shears, hence he follows a servile calling, and is not fit for literary or official

A CHINESE STUDENT.

honors. "But," they add triumphantly, "the toe-nail artist *must* sit when performing his duties, even in the presence and upon the person of the Emperor himself."

There are three regular degrees conferred upon successful candidates at the government examinations. The lowest gives the title of " Hsiu Tsai," or " Budding Talent ;" the second, of " Chu Jên," or " Promoted Man ;" and the third, that of " Chin Shih," or " Entered Scholar." They are sometimes compared with the Western titles, A.B., A.M., and LL.D., but there is absolutely no basis on which to establish any parallelism. There are three examinations which must be successfully passed in order to secure the lowest degree. These are held in the district and departmental cities. The examination for the second degree is held at the capital of the province, and occurs annually. That for the highest degree occurs but once each three years, and is held only at Peking. The examinations must be taken in order, and no candidate can enter for a higher degree until he has won the lower. He may try as often as he pleases, spend his entire life, as many do, in attempts and failures to secure the coveted degrees ; but he must take them in order, and is never debarred except for violation of some of the more serious of the numerous regulations under which the examinations are conducted.

The receipt of the lowest degree entitles its owner to be entered upon the list of prospective officeholders ; but if he has ambition for anything better than a subordinate position, he continues his studies either alone or under a coaching tutor, and seeks the highest literary honors before making any effort to enter political life. As has been said, many thus strive for a lifetime, and fail at last.

In every triennial examination at Peking—that at which the final honor is conferred—there is always a considerable sprinkling of old men. In one, the lists of which I saw, there was one candidate who was eighty-six years of age, and six who were more than seventy. In another, a candidate died in the course of the examination from fatigue and nervous excitement. He was eighty-eight years old. A posthumous degree was conferred upon him as a reward of persistency and virtuous ambition. By a special act of grace the Emperor confers the highest degree upon all candidates of good moral character who have won each degree but the last, and have tried for that and failed each three years until they have reached the age of ninety! It is hardly necessary to add that a degree thus conferred carries with it no right to an official appointment.

A lengthy article could be written upon the provisions and regulations under which these examinations are held. The most absolute care has been taken to render cheating, collusion, or any sort of trickery impossible. There are three separate sets of government officials connected with every examination. Before the first—the Board of Registration, as it may be called—the candidate is required to present himself, satisfy them that he is entitled to enter for that particular degree, and furnish them with a sealed envelope which contains a fictitious name which he has chosen, and which he is to endorse upon the essays written by him in the course of the test. When the candidates present themselves at the appointed hour to the second board—that having direct charge of the test—each one is subjected to a close personal search, and if a scrap of paper containing so much as a single written character is found upon him, he is at once bundled out of the enclosure in disgrace, and forever debarred from competition. Each is shut into a tiny cell, taking with him a few sheets of paper, writing apparatus, and a theme for an essay, which is handed him at the last moment. He is allowed to remain there about twenty hours, and is constantly watched by sentries to see that he has no communication with any other person. The preparation of several of these upon various themes, all selected from the Confucian classics, constitutes the examination. The papers are handed to a third body—the Board of Criticism—who make out the list of successful candidates by the fictitious names found upon each paper. Of course the writers are identified by means of the sealed envelopes deposited with the registrars. Theoretically the names of unsuccessful candidates are never known.

The examinations are conducted in the same manner and upon the same classes of topics for all the degrees. That they are rigid and exacting is shown by the fact that the average number who present themselves for each triennial examination at Peking is not far from fourteen thousand, while the average of those who pass is below fifteen hundred. As a rule, not more than ten per cent of those entered at any test secure the coveted degree. It is said that the scrutiny of the papers is mainly devoted to penmanship, literary style, orthodox Confucian ideas, and that any evidence of independent thought is sure of condemnation. They are certainly very severe upon the first two points named. A single error of the pen will cause a man to lose his degree, while a clear, concise style, combined with beautiful penmanship, is certain to bring high praise and rapid official promotion.

Where so many fail, it is not surprising that success is a matter of great congratulation to the fortunate man and his family. Feasts are given and much rejoicing is heard. After an examination large bills are placarded all about the streets of the city or town by successful candidates or their friends resident there, of one of which the following is a free translation : " Good news ! Mr. Wang has the happiness to announce that his son, Ah Sin, by the grace of His Imperial Majesty, has been named number 169 in the list of successful candidates for the degree of Master of Arts at the recent provincial examinations. Rejoice ! Rejoice !" And every one of Mr. Wang's and Ah Sin's friends go and call.

Little need be said here regarding Chinese literature. It is more voluminous than valuable, though, when the factor of false religious thought and superstitious idea is eliminated from it, the better portion of Chinese writing is found to rest upon a high moral basis. But those Oriental authors, however intellectual and talented they may have been, appear to have preferred to take some small theme and elaborate it to an infinitesimal point rather than to select a great subject and de-

CHINESE PONY AND GROOM.

velop it grandly. Their power lies in minuteness of detail. This is not surprising when it is remembered that the writings of Confucius form at once the centre, model, and type of all Chinese literary effort, and that any departure from these discredits and injures the author. There are a few excellent Chinese novels, but the bulk of their works of fiction is trash, and trash of the kind that is suppressed by the police.

Still the Chinese mind is full of wise and admirable sayings, quotations from their ancient and modern authors. Some of these bear a striking resemblance to familiar sayings in our own tongue.

Here are three or four of them :

"The poor are happy, the rich have many cares."

"If your children are wise, money will corrupt them ; if foolish, it will magnify their vices."

"Keep down the temper of the moment, and you will save a hundred days' anxiety."

"To the man who cares not for the future, troubles are nigh at hand."

"Consider the past and you will know the future."

"Riches spring from small beginnings, and poverty is the result of unthriftiness."

"Nine women in ten are jealous."

"Backbiting goes on from morning until night, but be deaf and it will die."

"Be friends with an official, and you will get poor ; with a merchant, and you will get rich ; with a priest, and you will get a subscription-book."

"There is no permanent feast on earth."

"The wise man is not talkative, nor the talker a sage."

"Study is the highest pursuit a man can follow."

"If your fields lie fallow, your granaries will be empty; if your books are not studied, your children will be fools."

CHAPTER XII.

ETIQUETTE AND CEREMONY.

Among the Chinese, etiquette may almost be said to take precedence of morality in importance. So far as rigid adherence to outward forms may go, as a nation they excel all others in the art of politeness. It is true that much of it has degenerated into mere mannerism. Still, the form survives, and makes up by the minuteness of detail and the rigidity of exaction what it lacks in spirit. The observance of these forms is practically universal. Cart-drivers on the streets, ragged and foul beggars by the roadside, country rustics and city fops—all alike practice and exact compliance with them. One may call a Chinese a liar, and, under many circumstances, he will accept the epithet as a well-deserved compliment; but either accuse him of a breach of etiquette or neglect any of the proper forms of speech due to him, and a quarrel will be the immediate result.

As might be expected in such an ancient country as China, the system of etiquette is not only thoroughly crystalized and fixed, it is also very complicated and tedious in its forms. It enters into the most minute detail of action and speech. To a large extent it deprives conversation of all freshness and originality by dictating a set form through which it may flow, and so covers simple questions between friends with a varnish or lacquer of extravagant adjectives and bombastic nouns, with fulsome compliment and intense but meaningless self-depreciation, as to render it absurd and silly. Take, for example, the following short dialogue, which is an exact translation of the invariable conversation which occurs between two gentlemen, or beggars for that matter, who meet for the first time :

"What is your honorable cognomen?"

"The trifling name of your little brother is Wang."

"What is your exalted longevity?"

"Very small Only a miserable seventy years."

"Where is your noble mansion?"

"The mud hovel in which I hide is in such or such a place."

"How many precious parcels [sons] have you?"

"Only so many stupid little pigs."

Of course in such a dialogue the various facts sought, all very simple, are given correctly ; but the formula of each question must be carefully preserved in this stilted fashion, and to omit a single flattering or depreciatory word would be noted as a breach of politeness, and hence as offensive. It is true that the spirit underlying such a conversation—that of deference—is good. It is that which leads each to prefer the other to himself ; but there is reason to believe that the spirit is gone from it, and that it is a mere shell of language, a form of words. Were this not the case, by such gross exaggeration it is made ridiculous and inane.

Among equals in China it is a gross breach of politeness to call a person by his given name. There are no exceptions to this rule. Between the closest friends or the nearest relatives the rule holds good. A Chinese would be angry if his twin brother addressed him in that manner. It must either be "Venerable elder brother" or "Venerable younger brother," as the facts warrant, and sons of the same mother have more than once been known to fall instantly to blows for no other reason than violation of this rule. They have a curious way of distinguishing the various sons in a family by numbers. Thus the eldest son of Mr. Jones would be called " Big Jones ;" the second, " Jones number 2 ;" the third, " Jones number 3." Persons of equal rank or station, outside the family, may either address them by the titles mentioned above, or as " Venerable Big Jones" or " Venerable Jones number 2," as the case may be. This is esteemed quite the correct thing ; but to address either of them by the family and given name would certainly give offense.

On the other hand, their superiors are expected, or at least are at liberty to use the given name, and are esteemed ignorant or boorish if they use the same form of address that their equals would employ ; and this fact furnishes the explanation to the peculiar etiquette mentioned above. The use of the given name is an offensive assumption of superiority. These minute discriminations, endless in number, often cause foreign residents to make absurd blunders in addressing their Chinese servants. One gentleman brought upon himself the ridicule of all the natives about him by invariably calling his porter by the title "Venerable elder brother." Knowing not a word of the language, and hearing other servants address the man by that title, he had, very naturally, concluded that it was his name. A member of a legation in Peking was seriously complained of because he had addressed the head of the Chinese Foreign Office as "Prince Kung" instead of "Venerable Prince," as he should have done according to Chinese etiquette. These blunders are sometimes more unfortunate than amusing, since by the Oriental, to whom the form of politeness is often more important than the substance, the foreigners who make them are regarded as boors and barbarians, and thus they may at times seriously affect important business.

Generally speaking, questions of etiquette have played a far more important part in the foreign relations of China, have produced more friction and misunderstanding than can readily be conceived. Chinese officials are exceedingly tenacious of their dignity. They have a minute and exact line of ceremony of intercourse among their own officials of varying ranks, and they strongly object, and perhaps naturally, to the payment of higher honors to a foreign official than would be conceded to a native of the same or corresponding rank. Thus, by way of illustration, the main entrance to every government office in China is provided with three doors: a central large door of two leaves and

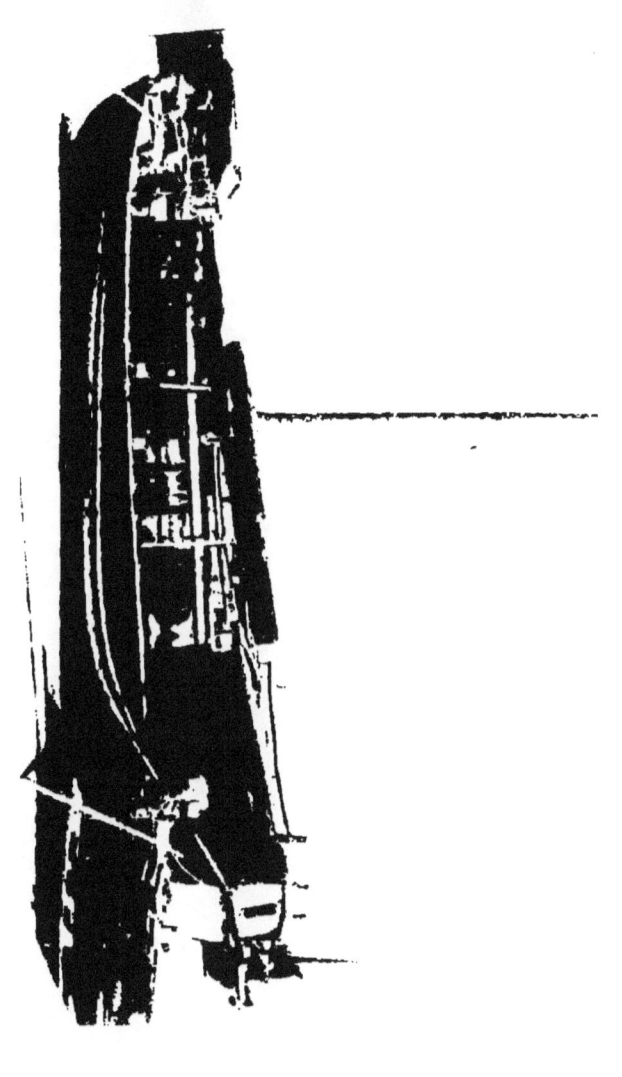

a smaller one of a single leaf on either side. It is a fixed rule among native officials that the great central door can only be opened for the passage of a person equal in rank with the head of the office. The consular representatives at Canton for many years had no interviews with the viceroy there because he declined to open the central door to his palace, and they declined to enter at either side door. Confessedly they were far below him in personal rank, but they insisted that it would be an affront to the dignity of the governments which they represented if they entered by any other than the great door. The question developed much vexatious diplomatic discussion, interfered for years with the transaction of business, but was finally disposed of by the concession of the point by the viceroy.

In a similar way the question of audience, about which so much has been written, and which was finally settled in 1873, after a discussion carried on almost daily for six months, was not a question of seeing or not seeing the Emperor. It was purely a question of ceremony. The Chinese never raised an objection to the interview, but they insisted that it should take place in accordance with the native ritual. From time immemorial, whenever a high officer of State, not excepting princes of the imperial lineage, have audience with the Emperor, they are required to perform what is known in the " Code of Etiquette" as the " three prostrations and nine knockings," commonly called the " kêtow." It consists in going upon the hands and knees three times, and each time knocking the forehead upon the floor three times. Not a very dignified or elegant ceremony, it must be confessed. The foreign representatives rightly refused to submit to this requirement of Chinese etiquette, upon the ground that it was alike degrading and unbecoming, since they were the official representatives of governments equal in rank and position with that of China, and also because it required of them the performance of an act to which they had never been asked to submit when presented to the rulers of their native lands. They would not render a greater act of subjection to a foreign ruler than they had ever granted to their own. The Chinese insisted upon the "kètow" for nearly six months, and only yielded upon being shown, by the American Minister, instructions directing him, in case the Chinese persisted, to break off relations and await further instructions, "which would be in accordance with the gravity of the situation." Then His Imperial Majesty gracefully yielded the point, and contented himself with the receipt of three profound bows. Two other minor points caused some discussion. The Chinese objected to the sword which forms an ornamental but useless part of every diplomatic uniform, since it is a most serious breach of propriety for a person bearing a weapon of any sort to enter the imperial presence. They also successfully attacked one of the representatives, who was practically blind when deprived of his eye-glasses. They appealed to his well-known good nature, and begged him to leave his spectacles at home, since it was grossly improper, from a Chinese standpoint, for any person to appear before the Emperor wearing them. He consented, and only found his way into the audience chamber by clinging to the arm of a colleague.

The etiquette surrounding the receipt and consumption of a cup of tea, simple as it may appear, has caused more than one foreigner to stumble, and, in one instance at least, produced vexatious results. An American gentleman had occasion to call upon a Chinese official about a matter of business, when it was very desirable that a good impression should be made. He was received with the most formal and ceremonious courtesy. Tea was brought in at once by a servant, and the official, taking a cup in both hands, raised it to his head, and then presented it in a most deferential manner to the foreigner. The Chinese host then seated himself, and a second cup was placed before him by the attendant. The guest, being thirsty after a long and dusty ride, seized his cup and swallowed the contents at a single draught. The manner of the Chinese official changed instantly, and from being most scrupulously polite and courteous, he became rude and insolent, would hear nothing about the business in hand, and the foreigner was sent out of his office almost as though he were a servant.

The guest had been guilty of two breaches of etiquette, both trivial in Western eyes, yet serious from a Chinese standpoint. In the first place, he should have received the cup of tea standing, when brought to him by his host. What was far more important, he should not have touched his tea, no matter how thirsty he might have been, until his host urged him to do so and set him the example, and he should have made that the signal of his departure. This part of the etiquette of tea-drinking is peculiar. Had the caller been equal or superior in rank to the host, he might have quenched his thirst whenever he saw fit; but being inferior to him, he was at liberty, according to Chinese rule, only to follow the motions of the host, who, on his part, would touch the tea when he wished the interview to end.

The official had never before met a foreigner, and hence was peculiarly on the watch to discover whether, from the Chinese point of view, he was a gentleman. The episode of the tea proved that he was not, and in consequence his visit was resented as an unwarranted and inexcusable intrusion.

It is impossible to overestimate the importance which the Chinese, of all ranks and classes, attach to these trifling details of etiquette, which indeed they consider as being essential parts of propriety of demeanor. It is easy to ignore them, but unwise if a person wishes to stand well with these Orientals, and doubly so if he desires to transact any important business with them. They measure the quality of a man by these apparently minute and trifling standards. They are taught to every school-boy, are as old as the nation, and as fixed as the hills. We may laugh at them, find them tedious and absurd, as, indeed, many of them are; yet they are an inherent part of the nation, and conformity to them, except in such as involve undignified or degrading acts, is essential to good-fellowship with the Chinese and to the successful accomplishment of any business to which they are parties. A volume might be written dedicated exclusively to illustrations of the evil results which have come from ignorant or willful violation of these rules of propriety, which, as has been said, are esteemed of equal or superior authority to the code of morals.

I once had occasion to dispatch a consul of the United States to the capital of an interior province to adjust some public business with the governor. The gentleman sent was the proud owner of a Mexican saddle, with its numberless and voluminous accoutrements. It may have been an article of beauty upon a large horse, but spread over the average undersized Chinese pony, it left little of the unfortunate animal visible except his beginning and end, his nose and tail. Thus fitted out, and provided with Mexican boots and spurs, a sombrero and a heavy riding-whip, the consular representative of the government of the United States reached the city of his destination in safety, having excited the animosity of every dog *en route* and the awe and superstitious fear of every celestial, who saw in him a new specimen of the animal creation. Half an hour after his arrival at the provincial capital, with a promptness highly commendable, if speed had been the only object desired, with the dust of a week's journey still upon his person, he sprang upon his pony, rattled over the paved streets of the city to the gate of the governor's palace, threw his bridle-rein, or his lariat, whichever it should be called, over a post, banged upon the great gate with the butt of his whip, and thrust his card into the hand of the dignified but astonished attendant. The governor refused to see him. He waited a week in the city, denied an opportunity to discuss his business with any official, and then set out on his return. He was mobbed in a city upon his homeward journey. The business entrusted to him was very seriously complicated by this unseemly performance, and dragged on the wearisome round of diplomatic correspondence for three more years. In order to complete the illustration, and to show the importance of conformity to Chinese etiquette, it ought to be added that at the end of that time I visited the same city upon the same errand. I was received with excessive courtesy and kindness by the same governor, and concluded the business to my entire satisfaction at the first interview. The consul could have done the same had he shown a reasonable degree of deference to Chinese rules of propriety. The difference lay not in the men, but in the manner.

Whenever two Chinese acquaintances, either riding on horseback, being driven in carts, or carried in chairs, meet, each is expected to dismount and make his salutations to the other. Each must hasten to be first upon the ground, each must urge the other not to alight, and each must insist that the other shall be the first to remount. And they do all this with the greatest apparent eagerness and sincerity; yet it is only rigmarole and play-acting. Each knows which should descend and which remount first, and woe betide the other if he yields to his friend's show of entreaty, and either fails to dismount first, or returns to his carriage while his superior in years or station is standing in the street. His acquaintances would fail to recognize him, and his reputation as a gentleman would be gone forever.

Yet there is much human nature left in the cultivated Chinese, and with them, while a tedious or inconvenient rule of polite conduct is never openly ignored or violated, it is almost uniformly evaded; and the direct result of this cumbersome ceremonial is that Chinese gentlemen, who never walk, always fail to see their friends upon the street. If in carts or chairs, the curtains are closely drawn; if on horseback, they are always looking in another direction. I have known a Chinese official to bow most politely to me as we met, and at the same moment to fail to recognize an Oriental friend and associate, whom he had met almost daily for forty years. They were close friends; but while he was at liberty to follow the foreign style of recognition with me, he was bound by another and more laborious code of etiquette regarding the other. Hence the difference in his conduct toward us.

· There is the same tedious and absurd formula to be observed whenever several persons enter or leave a room together, or seat themselves at table. Each knows perfectly his own place, fixed by his rank relative to the others, and hence he knows which will finally enter or leave the room first, have the higher seat at the table, and take and leave that first. The rule is absolute and univer-

sally understood, and no deviation from it would
be tolerated ; yet each one crowds back and urges
another to take the precedence, and the friendly
struggle must last for several minutes before the
various members of the party accept their proper
places. If time were of any importance in China,
as it never appears to be, the loss involved in these
fictitious contests would amount to something
quite serious. Take, as a specimen, a visit to the
Chinese Foreign Office. I went there one day to
speak with the ministers. Two were present when
I arrived, and received me. We struggled about
the doorway before we could enter in proper order,
and again at the circular table, at which business
is always transacted, before we could take our
seats. During the interview, five other ministers
came in, one at a time. With each arrival those
already present hurried outside the door and struggled in again, and then quarreled kindly for the
lowest seat at the table. A considerable amount
of time was wasted in this farce, and the order of
the persons about the table was changed five times
in two hours.

Much of the falsehood to which the Chinese as
a nation are said to be addicted is a result of the
demands of etiquette. A plain, frank "no" is the
height of discourtesy. Refusal or denial of any
sort must be softened and toned down into an expression of regretted inability. Unwillingness to
grant a favor is never shown. In place of it there
is seen a chastened feeling of sorrow that unavoid-
able but quite imaginary circumstances render it
wholly impossible. Centuries of practice in this

form of evasion have made the Chinese matchlessly fertile in the invention and development of excuses. It is rare, indeed, that one is caught at

THE DONKEY.

a loss for a bit of artfully embroidered fiction with which to hide an unwelcome truth.

The same remark holds good in regard to all

manner of disagreeable subjects of conversation. They must be avoided. Any number of winding paths may be made around them, but none must ever go directly through. A Chinese very seldom will make an intentionally disagreeable or offensive remark. If he is dissatisfied he does not say so, but leaves the person to infer the dissatisfaction and to search out the cause, while he is listening to some tale which has been invented with a view to accomplish the same purpose which an expression of the bare fact would secure, but by more pleasant means. If a Chinese servant is not pleased with his work or wages, he never complains. That would be excessively rude; but he at once kills his father or stretches his brother upon a bed of sickness, all in his imagination, and announces the sorrowful tidings as a cause for leaving service. If his master is a foreigner, and not well versed in Oriental ways, he probably accepts the statement as true, condoles with him, much to his disgust, and, perhaps, loses a valuable servant; but if he is accustomed to the Chinese methods of indirection, beyond expressing regret at the misfortune recited to him, he takes no action until he has learned from another employé the actual cause of dissatisfaction. Then he deals with it according to circumstances, always, however, keeping up the farce of the fictitious affliction. To bring the negotiation down to the basis of fact would cause his servant to "lose face," to be put to shame, and then no increase of wages would persuade him to remain.

The extent to which the Chinese will go in order

to cover up disagreeable truths, and the efforts they will make to disguise their real feelings and motives, are simply astonishing. This is equally true of all grades and classes. The highest officials or the most cultivated scholars are not more expert or uniform in their obedience to the exactions of this rule of propriety than the meanest coolie. If they are obliged to announce an event unwelcome to them, it is done in a tone and manner meant to carry the impression that they regard it as utterly trivial and unimportant. I have known a Chinese to mention the death of his only son with a laugh, as though it was of not the least consequence; yet, as a matter of fact, it was in his opinion the greatest misfortune that could have befallen him. Only in private, and to his closest friends, would his sense of dignity and the demands of etiquette allow him to uncover his heart and show his actual grief.

This habit of repression and misrepresentation of feeling has given the outside world the idea that, as a nation, the Chinese are stolid, indifferent, and lacking in nerves. Such is not the case. They are keenly sensitive, proud, and passionate. As might be expected, when, under a provocation too great for endurance, they give way to their feelings, the result, whether it be grief or anger, is as extreme and unreasonable, from our standpoint, as their ordinary suppression of emotion is absurd and unnecessary. It is difficult, perhaps unfair, to judge them in this regard, since their standard is absolutely different from ours. They have covered themselves with a lacquer of courtesy

and etiquette so thick and highly polished that
the real fibre of character lying underneath is discovered
only upon very rare occasions. Half the
world believes that the lacquer covers nothing
valuable, or containing the finer qualities of manhood.
The fact that his intense exhibitions of
passion are called out by what are to us trivial
causes, only serves to intensify this mistaken opinion.
A Chinaman is grossly insulted, and he
laughs. A moment later some one carelessly treads
upon his toe, and, in an instant, he gives way to
an uncontrollable fit of rage. His anger seems
childish, and his reception of the insult unmanly.
While both of these adjectives may be justly applied
in particular cases, it is, after all, only when
we know the laws of self-restraint, the canons of
propriety, which have governed him for ages, and
judge him by those laws, that we can reach any
fair estimate of him as a man to-day.

Nothing so confuses and disconcerts the Chinese
as the blunt and outspoken way in which Western
people, especially Americans and the English, express
their opinions, or seek to accomplish any desired
object. They cover up their designs as
closely and as modestly as we do our bodies. We
expose ours naked; and if, in intercourse with
them, we are often puzzled to the point of exasperation
to discover what it is, so carefully wrapped
and concealed, that they actually desire, they, on
the other hand, are not infrequently misled by
our frankness, and give us what we wish, chuckling
with the mistaken thought that it was not what we
wanted, but that our apparently naked purpose

was, after all, only a cloak covering another and quite different design.

The following incident illustrates another phase or branch of the complicated system of Chinese etiquette. In January, 1881, the butler employed by the writer, and who had been in his service some ten years, informed him that he must leave his position. Upon being asked for his reason, he stated that on the previous evening he had gone out after dinner, and had thoughtlessly locked the room which he and the fireman occupied together, and had taken the key with him. The fireman was also out, and, upon coming home about eleven o'clock, was, of course, unable to enter his room.

He could easily have gone into a room with another servant for the night, but refused to do so, because very angry, and going to the residence of the butler's family near by, he had worked himself into a violent passion, raved and stormed up and down the street, calling the butler's wife and mother all manner of evil names, and had effectually roused the entire neighborhood.

Having performed in this manner for about an hour, he returned to the Legation and went to bed with another servant, as he ought to have done in the first place. The butler added that the offense was so serious and so public, that he had decided to "take the law" to the fireman, and as it would not be decent to take such a step when both remained in the master's service, he must beg to be released.

I pointed out to him, in the first place, that no Chinese court could take notice of his complaint so long as the fireman remained in the service of an officer of the Legation ; hence, it would be idle for him to give up his position unless the fireman were also discharged. In the second place, I pointed out to him that to take the matter into the courts would only serve to let five hundred people hear the bad words used, when not more than fifty people had heard them in the first instance. I promised to look into the matter carefully, and if the facts were as stated, to see that the fireman was properly dealt with. I urged the butler not to leave his place, and not to take any further steps until I had made an effort to settle the difficulty. To this, after some hesitation, the butler consented.

The writer then sent for the fireman, and asked for his side of the story. Strangely enough, it agreed entirely with what the butler had said. The fireman admitted that he was entirely in the wrong, said he was very much ashamed of what he had done, and promised to submit to any punishment which the master saw fit to inflict. He was spoken to very sharply about his offense, and told plainly that had he been a foreigner, his words, if used toward the family of another foreigner, would possibly have cost him his life.

After allowing the matter to rest two or three days, the butler and fireman were summoned before the master and their fellow-servants. The master recited the facts, which both admitted to be correct.

CHINESE MULE LITTER.

The fireman then confessed his fault, and went upon his hands and knees before the butler, knocking his head three times upon the floor by way of begging pardon. He was then sent with the butler and another servant to the butler's house, where he made a similar apology to the wife and mother whom he had insulted. This was the Chinese way of settlement, and with it the writer supposed the trouble had ended, as the injured party said he was satisfied.

But two days later the butler came to his master again to say that while he and his family were satisfied with the apology made, yet the insulting words had been shouted in the ears of all the neighbors, who knew nothing about the fireman's confession and apology, and that the neighbors were already looking askance at him, and, to quote the exact words used by him, " unless he could find some way to repaint his front door"—that is, find some way to make the fireman's apology public—the neighbors would refuse to have anything to do with him, and might drive him out of the neighborhood.

The writer admitted the force of this point, and, after a moment's thought, said :

" Well, I think you are right ; and I will fine the fireman half a month's wages, and pay you the money. Then you can tell your neighbors that I have done so. Here is the money, and I will take it out of his wages at the end of the month."

Three dollars were handed to the butler.

But he refused them, saying : " Oh, no ; I can't do that. It would only make the matter worse.

The neighbors would then say that I had allowed my family to be insulted for three dollars."

"Well, what shall I do with the case?"

The butler replied: "Give the money to one of the other servants, telling him what it is for, and he will know how to use it."

This was done. The money was given to the groom, who was told to use it in whatever manner he thought best, to satisfy the neighbors of the butler that the fireman had made due reparation. The writer presumed that the money would be spent for a feast, to which the neighbors would be invited, and at which the fireman would publicly repeat his confession and apology.

But three days later the groom came to his master and said:

"I have attended to that matter which you gave me. I paid a dollar and forty cents for paint, and a dollar for a painter. The work has been done, and I have sixty cents left. What shall I do with it?"

The writer, astonished beyond measure, said:

"I don't understand you. What do you mean about paint and a painter?"

The groom explained then that the butler had meant literally what he had said about "repainting his front door;" that it was a custom in Peking that, in similar cases of insult to the members of a family, the front door should be freshly painted at the expense of the person guilty of the insult, as a public act of apology and retraction. Hence, he had caused the butler's door to have a new coat of paint, and thus public opinion was satisfied and the insulted dignity and wounded honor of the butler were avenged!

The groom was directed to return the sixty cents, cash balance in hand, to the fireman.

CHAPTER XIII.

MERCHANTS AND TRICKS OF TRADE.

WHILE there is no such thing as caste in China, and few class distinctions more fixed and permanent than those current in the United States, the entire population is divided and ranked in public estimation according to the occupation of each individual. This gradation is expressed in the phrase, "Shih, nung, kung, shang," which every Chinese uses, and which expresses exactly the comparative estimation in which the various callings are held, beginning with the highest and grading downward. Translated into English, it runs thus: "Scholars, farmers, artisans or laborers, merchants."

This arrangement is not so unphilosophic as may at first sight appear. Scholars rank highest in the social order, since the brain is better than the body. The producer comes next in honor, because he alone is able to develop something out of nothing, or, at least, approximates as closely to that result as any human being can. The artisan or laborer ranks third, since he, by hand and brain, transforms a less valuable article into one of more general utility and adapted to a higher range of service. The merchant stands at the bottom of the list, for the reason that he neither produces nor increases the inherent value or usefulness of anything. He trades upon the labor and the needs of others. He is simply a medium of interchange. Right or wrong, this is the Chinese view; and the four words are used in a broad generic sense. The first comprises all educated men, thus embracing all officials; the second embraces all tillers of the soil; the third, all forms of skilled and unskilled labor; and the fourth, the entire and immense variety of commercial occupations.

However Chinese merchants may be catalogued in the social grades of their native land, they have no occasion to fear the results of comparison with their fellows in other parts of the world. They are shrewd, sagacious, enterprising, and, as a class, upright and honorable. They realize fully the importance of a reputation for commercial integrity, and scrupulously maintain their credit. As has been justly said by a recent English writer, "The merchants and traders of China have gained the respect and won the admiration of all those who have been brought into contact with them." A few years since the manager of the largest foreign banking house in the most important commercial centre of the East said, in speaking upon this point: "I have referred to the high commercial standing of the foreign community. The Chinese are in no way behind us in that respect—in fact, I know of no people in the world I would sooner trust than the Chinese merchant and banker. I may mention that for the last twenty-five years the bank has been doing a very large business with Chinese, amounting to hundreds of millions of taels (ounces of silver bullion), and we have never yet met with a defaulting Chinaman." And it ought to be added that no man in either the Eastern or Western world was so well qualified to express an opinion upon this point as the gentleman whose remarks are here quoted.

Many causes have combined to produce this desirable result, one of which deserves especial mention. There are three "settling days" in each year for all classes of business transactions in the Chinese Empire. Accounts may, by mutual consent, be carried past two of these, and sometimes are; but on New Year's Day every transaction must be put into exact shape, the books balanced, and all debts paid. That this rule is on rare occasions violated or compromised is doubtless true, but not to any such extent as to render it less than certain and imperative. In certain sections of the empire money-lenders are required, if called upon to do so, to rebate a certain percentage of the interest accrued and payable if the debt is paid within the last ten days of the old year; but this concession is rarely claimed by any except the very poor, since it lessens their ability to secure loans in the future. Custom demands that any respectable Chinese having business out of doors after dark should carry a lantern, no matter if there be a full moon shining in a cloudless sky. As a result of this peculiar badge of respectability, the streets of any Chinese city present a curious sight upon New Year's morning. Well-dressed Orientals may be

CHINESE JINRICKSHA.

seen hurrying about in the full blaze of the morning sun, carrying a bundle of bills in one hand and a lighted lantern in the other. To them it is theoretically New Year's Eve. Only when the last bill is paid or collected does the first day of the new year dawn. Then the lantern is extinguished, and they recognize the existence of the sunlight.

The Chinese are what may be termed natural merchants. Possessing the commercial instinct in a high degree, they are close, shrewd, and far-sighted in their bargains, untiring in their efforts to get the better of those with whom they deal, and fertile to an astonishing degree in the "tricks of the trade." They understand as well as the sharpest Western merchant that a positive advantage may sometimes be gained by selling an article at less than its actual cost. A Chinese who kept a small hotel in Peking—and he was a merchant in the native sense of the word—once applied this principle in a very peculiar fashion. He asked at the United States Legation for information whether, according to our laws, he could eject a non-paying American boarder from his establishment, and hold the debtor's baggage as security for his bill. He was informed that he could, but advised, if he decided to dismiss his unprofitable guest, to allow him to take his property away, since it could not be worth more than "two dollars and a half."

"That may be true," he replied, "but two dollars and a half is more than nothing. The fact is," he added, "when this man first came to me I agreed to let him have board and lodging for a dollar a day. He remained six months with me upon those terms, but paid me nothing. Then I reduced the price to half a dollar a day in order that I might not lose so much by him." This incident is given rather as an Oriental vagary than as an example of shrewdness.

There are some very essential differences between the Chinese retail merchant or trader, as our British friends would call him, and his *confrère* in the Western world. The foreign merchant studies the cost of his merchandise, its quality, the condition of the market, whether supply is in excess of demand or the reverse, and fixes his price accordingly.

The Chinese trader studies all these points with equal care, but he also studies each customer. He looks him over from head to foot, makes a rapid but generally accurate estimate as to his character, his closeness or generous hand in making a bargain, his knowledge or ignorance of the ruling price, and only when he has completed his studies upon these points does he inform the purchaser what the desired article will cost him. Thus the price depends quite as much upon the buyer as upon the actual value of the merchandise. A foreigner always pays more for any given article than a Chinese, and a foreigner who cannot speak the native tongue pays for his ignorance at the rate of from ten to a hundred per cent increase in the cost of anything he may purchase.

I stood once at a fair or market in the edge of a circle of Chinese who were buying bunches of violets from a wrinkled old Chinese gardener. He was disposing of his flowers quite rapidly at two pieces of cash. After watching the scene for a few moments, I made my way through the crowd and asked the old man the price of his violets. "Thirty-six pieces of cash a bunch," he replied, without hesitating an instant. "You robber," said I, "here you have been selling them for two pieces of cash to these people, and now you wish me to pay eighteen times as much!" "Oh," he replied, "you speak Chinese, do you? I did not know that. Then you can have them for two cash, the same as though you were a Chinaman." And he joined heartily in the laugh of the crowd at the failure of his little scheme to secure an exorbitant price.

One peculiar result of this study of a customer is seen in the fact that if a person enters a store in China, and, after examining several articles, asks the price of any one of them, unless it is positively known that he has spoken to but one clerk, no answer will be made by him to whom the question is put until every other clerk has been asked if he has named a price for the article in question to the gentleman. If, as very rarely happens, this important precaution is neglected, the sums named by different clerks will almost invariably be unlike, thus showing that they fail to agree in their estimates of the customer.

I once caught two clerks napping in this respect, with the amazing result that the first asked five dollars for an article barely worth two, and five minutes later the second gravely declared that the firm had decided to sell that particular piece of merchandise at a loss, and hence only charged fifteen dollars for it!

Another illustration of the fact that the Chinese grade their charges according to their customers would be found in an examination of the prices paid by foreigners for such common articles of food as beef and mutton. Every one pays more than his Chinese neighbors—probably no two pay exactly the same price; or if the nominal rate per pound is the same, the number of ounces given for a pound will not be quite the same. The solitary barber in Peking who understands the foreign mode of hair-dressing charges a foreign minister half a dollar; a secretary of legation, twenty five cents; and an unofficial foreigner, ten cents. The native pays about half a cent for the same service. Water-carriers and scavengers grade their monthly bills in a similar manner.

In passing through Japan I once had occasion to employ a Chinese chiropodist residing there. His charges, so he declared, were five cents to his fellow-Chinese, ten cents to an ordinary Japanese, and half a dollar to all other foreigners. In the course of the inevitable conversation which took place, the Chinaman said:

"I hear that our Chinese minister came to this hotel to-day. Do you know whom he came to see?"

"Oh, yes," said I; "he came to call upon me."

"Then you must be an official," said the Chinaman, "otherwise he would not have visited you."

I modestly admitted such to be the fact. The conversation then drifted to other subjects. When his labors were concluded he demanded a dollar in payment, in the face of the assertion that his regular charge to all foreigners, excepting Japanese, was fifty cents ; and he enforced his claim by this argument in " pidgin English" : " Sposey that China minister come see you, you b'long all same he. You b'long same he, you makey pay one dollar all same. That b'long ploper."

An essential feature of every Chinese commercial transaction, no matter how great or how trivial, is the dicker. A bargain is, in fact, an intellectual duel, entered upon with all the eager watchfulness and determination of the knights of old. What eloquence, what vigor of expression, what freedom of gesture one may there see expended over the price or *weight* of two pounds of cabbage, a cold boiled sweet potato, or a cucumber ! Quotations from the Confucian classics, impassioned appeals to bystanders, arguments based on justice and reason, and irreverent and uncomplimentary allusions to the ancestors of the other man—all these come in play over a question which involves less than one cent.

Each is seeking an advantage over the other, and frequently each is successful, the buyer paying less than the usual price and the seller balancing the account by giving him short weight or measure. Hence each is happy. At a fish market, for example, one may see a dignified, well-dressed Chinese gentleman duly armed with steelyards, the bar being graded to weigh three different sorts of pounds, none exact, but each too heavy, engaged in a bargain for a carp. The fish has been selected from a dozen which were swimming about

in a tub of water. It has been weighed by the
buyer's steelyards, which are too heavy, and by
the fisherman's, which are too light. The first
display of eloquence arises over the weight, there
being, in a fair-sized fish, probably a difference of
a pound and a half between them. This is finally
adjusted by mutual compromise, subject, however,
to revision if they cannot otherwise agree upon
the price per pound ; and over this point the war
of words is renewed, and rages more furiously than
ever. Each has much to say about his concession
upon the point of the weight. Each assures the
other that it is really not a matter of any consequence ; that the few cash involved would not cause
him to waste a moment or a single word, but that
the broad and eternal principles of justice are at
stake, and that he is their champion and defender ;
and appeals to righteousness, truth, and Heaven
fly thick and fast, until, each hoarse and out of
breath, some further compromise is reached, and
the bargain concluded.

And, after all, it is only fair to say that it is
more for the pleasure of the argument, the exercise of the lungs and vocal organs, and, above all,
the satisfaction of having won a concession—it is
more for these than for the sum involved that
these contests are waged. A Chinese merchant
would be bitterly disappointed, and consider that
he had been defrauded of his just rights, if the
price named by him for any commodity were accepted without demur or debate ; and any Chinaman who accepted the first price would be held as
a fool by his countrymen.

It is considered a breach of good manners to ask the price of an article without the intention of making a purchase, and equally discourteous, upon hearing the price named, to pass on without argument or remonstrance concerning it.

"What is the price of that piece of felt?" asked a passer-by of a merchant selling squares of the article upon the street.

"Twenty-five tiao," replied the vendor.

"Ugh!" said the inquirer, who then walked away. The merchant gazed after him for a few moments, and then suddenly broke out into a torrent of most abusive language, calling the would-be buyer and all his relatives by the foulest and most offensive names. The object of this abuse walked more slowly, then stopped, hesitated, turned about, came back, and by the time he reached the felt merchant he, too, was in furious anger, and a battle seemed imminent.

"What do you mean by calling me names?" he demanded.

"What do you mean by asking the price of my goods and then going away without a civil word?" retorted the merchant.

"What made you ask me such a price?"

"Well, what if I did? You are a good Son of Han, and you ought to know that we don't do business in any such way. If all men acted as you did, no bargains would ever be made. You should have expostulated with me, and then we would have discussed the matter together. That is the only proper way. You know well enough that the price first named never means anything."

Thereupon the passer-by duly expostulated, the pair were shortly in an excited discussion over the proper value of the square of felt, and in a short time a bargain was concluded.

It may be said, in passing, that this love for a dicker is most deeply rooted in the Chinese character, and shows itself everywhere and at all times. Whether it is a coolie buying a cucumber or the heads of the government negotiating a treaty of vast importance, less is offered than will eventually be given, and more is demanded than is seriously expected or desired. Room is left upon both sides for a concession ; and a certain amount of this byplay invariably precedes the serious and practical part of the transaction. The Emperor Kang Hsi declared in the sacred edicts that the word "jang," meaning to yield, to concede, to compromise, was the most important word in the Chinese language, since it lies at the root of all harmonious and kindly relations. The entire nation appears to have absorbed this idea, and to put it into practice in every phase and act of life.

The lack of laws, or of their enforcement for standard weights and measures, goes far to open opportunities for discussion as well as to allow the practice of tricks and deceptions in every line of business. Steelyards are regularly made and sold in the markets, having two sets of pounds measured upon them, one to be used in buying and the other in selling. In various grades of cotton-wool a varying number of ounces to the pound is used. For the coarse grades the purchaser receives sixteen ounces, or a full pound ; for medium qualities, only twelve ounces, while in the very finest he receives twenty-one ounces to the pound. Cloths of all sorts are sold by the foot. The merchant invariably uses one foot when he buys, and a shorter one when he sells. The foot used for cotton goods is longer than that for woolen, which in turn exceeds that used in measuring silk. Such variations, regularly established by custom, necessarily counterbalance themselves, since the price must be adjusted to suit the varying measure. Beyond serving as traps to catch the unwary, and furnishing opportunities for discussion, they serve no purpose whatever. No Chinaman has ever been discovered who could explain their origin or give any reason for their continuance save that one—which is all-powerful with the Oriental—their antiquity.

To the Western mind these irregularities are as absurd and irrational as many other customs which exist in the Chinese Empire, and which are undisturbed and reverenced in spite of their inconvenience solely because they date back to the beginning of time. I was surprised in driving into an inn-yard one day, in the western part of China, to find several large stacks of second-hand cart-axles scattered about. Inquiry as to their use developed the fact that the gauge of the road changed at that particular spot, being six inches wider west of the inn than to the east of it. There was absolutely no reason for the change in the topography of the country or in any other condition of travel. Yet there stood the inexplicable and unreasonable fact that every wheeled vehicle, having come, perhaps, hundreds of miles upon the great imperial highway, must, upon entering that insignificant yard in a village of not fifty houses, exchange its axle for one of broader or narrower gauge, according as it was proceeding east or west; and the only explanation possible to be given was that "carts always had changed axles at that inn." The preservation of the antique is a ruling passion, and a reason above reason and logic in the Chinese mind.

It is evident that, with a varying system of weights and measures, and a currency that is flexible and elastic rather than definite in value, a large element of uncertainty must exist in all forms of business. Exact bookkeeping is an impossibility, and the merchant can only reach an approximate estimate of his gains or losses in any particular transaction or in his trade for a given period. But the Chinaman is more of a philosopher than a mathematician. He delights in broad generalities rather than in accurate statements, and so long as he is moderately prosperous in his enterprises, the large increase of the speculative element thrown into them by the peculiar features mentioned only add charm and fascination to his calling. A bargain ceases to be a dull, prosaic transfer of one commodity in exchange for another. It is always a contest of wits and often a battle royal, in which the keenest mind wins the victory. A Chinese will insist that any dolt can measure off so many exact lengths of cloth and receive for them a specified number of pieces of silver. To him such a transaction is dull, stupid, and flat, requiring neither art, tact, nor skill. Then he adds—and in this he is right—that only a man can carry a bargain to a successful conclusion in his country.

One interesting feature in the commercial world of China is the co-operative system which is in universal operation. Every member of an establishment, from the senior partner down to the boy who furnishes each customer with the inevitable cup of tea, or who sweeps the floor and runs on errands, has his share of the profits. The percentages are carefully graded to correspond with the position of the various clerks and employés; but every one has a personal interest in enlarging the business and in increasing its prosperity. As a rule, partners and their subordinates live together, generally in the store or office, eat at a common table, and thus form one family. No argument is needed to demonstrate the advantages of such a system. The entire staff is bound together by a common purpose, which affects each directly and personally. Distracting or unfriendly influences are either destroyed or reduced to harmless proportions.

The co-operative principle has another and peculiar form of application in China, which, though less desirable, is of equally general application. No chapter upon the commercial side of Chinese life would be complete if it failed to describe the most serious of all " tricks of trade," that commonly known among foreigners resident there as " the squeeze."

The Chinese " squeeze" is not exactly the embrace of affection nor the close grasp of hands joined in friendship. It is purely a business term, and refers to a pressure exerted upon money in any form by the fingers of every man through whose hands it may pass, but to whom it does not belong—a pressure which causes a portion of the coin to remain in his possession. It is a recognized but unallowed commission. The sufferers by the system call it stealing, while those who profit by it regard the sums gained as entirely legitimate perquisites, which they are fully entitled to receive.

The Chinese in their dealings with each other all suffer from and all practice it. The system is as old as the empire, and is said to owe its origin to an ancient custom under which household servants were paid no regular wages, but received food, one suit of clothes each year, and a sum of money provided in the following manner. From the price of every article of whatever sort used in the family, the porter at the gate retained one piece of cash in every fifty. Three times a year the amount thus secured was distributed among the servants in proportion to their positions in the service of the family. As all Chinese houses are built in an enclosure surrounded by a high wall with but a single entrance, at which a porter is in attendance at all hours, enforcement of such a practice would be easy, and the man at the gate would naturally act as collector. It is easy for him to know all the purchases made in the " compound," as it is called ; and if a merchant declined to pay the squeeze demanded, he would be refused admission. Whether this explanation is correct or

CHINESE SERVANTS.

not cannot be positively asserted. It is, however, a fact that, in paying or receiving cash, one gives or gets only forty-nine pieces for each nominal fifty, unless a special agreement for "full cash" has been made.

There is no incongruity in bringing Chinese servants into a chapter devoted to commercial affairs. They make nearly all the purchases in every establishment with which they are connected, and are merchants within the native meaning of that broad and elastic word. As a class they are probably the best in the world. They are quiet, prompt, faithful, and attentive. They seldom complain of late hours or hard work. They have a keen sense of responsibility, and are exceptionally honest. Table linen, silverware, jewelry, valuable bric-à-brac, and money may be left in their charge with confidence that every piece will be faithfully accounted for. In fifteen years, with a large establishment of servants, I never had occasion to charge one with theft, or with the loss through carelessness of any article. It is commonly and truly remarked that ladies who have lived in China are spoiled for housekeeping at home by the excellent service to which they have become accustomed.

But honest and faithful as they are in every other respect, Chinese servants will squeeze, and much of their diligence and promptness, much of their good nature and patience under hard work and late hours, is due to this practice. They never complain of much company, extra labor, or any unusual demands upon them. They simply "charge it in the bill." They have, on the other hand, been known to leave situations because the family lived too quietly and had too small an account at the grocer's. With all the varying expressions of jollity, frankness, or stupidity seen upon their faces, they are shrewd students of human nature. Each could tell if he would all the foibles and weaknesses of his master, and especially how far he may safely be bled, and at what point the squeezing process must stop.

The system of "the squeeze" is universal. All sorts of devices and expedients have been resorted to by foreign residents in China to put an end to it, and all have failed. If one does his own marketing and makes all his purchases in person, he soon discovers that his servants have quietly followed him up and levied a commission upon every person with whom he has dealt. He also discovers that, allowing nothing for the time spent, his servants can buy more cheaply than he, even when their squeeze is added to the proper market price. Thus he has lost not only time, but money, in his effort at reform.

If he takes pains to inform himself upon the proper prices of all articles used, the servant deceives him in weight or measure, charging for five pounds when he has bought only four. Then perhaps the master provides himself with Chinese scales and measures by which he tests every purchase. He is then happy until he discovers that his scales weigh only fourteen ounces to the pound, and that he is consequently paying a squeeze of twelve and one half per cent. Determined not to be beaten, the employer procures a pair of steelyards that have been tested and found to be full weight. These are kept under lock and key, and at last he is confident that the last chance for deception has vanished. Again he is mistaken. He has, it is true, weighed his pound of mutton, found it full weight, and for it paid only the market price ; but after this was done, and the master had turned away, the cook cut off a good-sized piece from the joint, which he returned to the butcher, and for which he received payment.

An acquaintance who had tried all the expedients given here, and who yet was suspicious that, in some inconceivable way, he was still being circumvented, summoned his cook to the dining-room one day and called his attention to the extremely small size of the joint of roast mutton upon the table. To this the cook, grave and dignified, with the utmost deference in tone and manner, replied : " Your Excellency is quite correct. The joint does seem small ; but your Excellency should not fail to make allowance for the fact that, in a dry climate like Peking, mutton shrinks much more in roasting than in your honorable country."

The dismissal of a servant found guilty of this practice rarely serves any good purpose. It may, indeed, be found later that his successor is worse, not merely making his own modest profit, but paying a pension to the man discharged. In one of the Legations in Peking years ago the minister determined to suppress the practice, and dismissed the porter, or gatekeeper, who, as has been said, is an important actor in the system. Long afterward it was discovered that the other servants, headed by the new gatekeeper, had regularly paid the discharged servant his usual wages up to the day of his death, and had then buried him with much ceremony and expense. They had a book-keeper and an account at a bank where all "squeezes" were deposited. Dividends were declared three times each year.

Arguments with the Chinese to prove the essential immorality of this custom are useless. It is a time-honored institution, which may be kept within moderate proportions by a little care and watchfulness, but which cannot be wholly suppressed, at least until the entire fabric of Oriental character is changed. Chinese suffer from the practice far more than foreigners, since the latter would never hesitate to make proper inquiries as to prices of articles in use ; but the dignity which surrounds a Chinese official allows the exercise of no such precautions. Hence he is simply a helpless victim, to be squeezed without limit or fear of results.

It may be said that the many devices and tricks which have been hinted at rather than described as characteristic of Chinese merchants are not at all consonant with the high character for integrity and upright dealing given them in the earlier part of the chapter. An answer to such a criticism is easily found. Human nature is much the same the world over. China is not alone in the possession of a large class of men who are scrupulous in the performance of every business obligation—men who may safely be trusted to any extent, whose word has all the validity of an oath, and yet who will not hesitate to resort to the pettiest tricks and schemes to increase their profits. Men are often great in great affairs, but fearfully small and mean in little things.

CHAPTER XIV.

THE POOR IN CHINA.

THE opinion, sometimes expressed, that the Chinese are a very rich people is quite erroneous. While the empire is rich in undeveloped resources and capabilities, the masses of the population are poor with a poverty of which we have only a faint conception. The average of wealth to each person in the United States is many times greater than in China. The word "poverty" does not convey at all the same idea in the two countries. In America a man is called poor who has a family to support upon earnings of, perhaps, two dollars a day. In China such a man would be looked upon as living in the very lap of luxury. Here, when the laboring man cannot afford meat twice daily, he and those dependent upon him are supposed to be upon the verge of hardship and destitution. Meat is cheaper there than here, yet a laborer there, receiving what he considers good wages, cannot afford to eat a pound in a month. Poverty here means a narrow and limited supply of luxuries. There it means actual hunger and nakedness, if not starvation within sight.

Of course in China, as in all other lands, there

is a close and necessary connection between the cost of food and the price of labor. If wages are very low, the cost of such articles of food as are absolutely necessary to sustain life and furnish strength to do a given amount of work must be correspondingly reduced, or death from starvation is the immediate result. The Chinese do not live poorly because they desire nothing better. Like all other men, they live as well as their earnings or resources will allow. A wealthy Chinaman dresses as expensively, though in a different style, has a table as luxurious, though his taste may be esteemed peculiar, and generally maintains the same elegance as his Western brother. There, as everywhere else, the income must control the expense.

Skilled laborers in China earn from ten to thirty cents in silver each day, the average coming below twenty. Unskilled laborers, or men who, in the expressive language of the country, "sell their strength," earn from five to ten cents each day, the average not rising above seven. This meagre sum, in a country where bachelors and old maids are unknown, must furnish the entire support of the man himself, and from one to four or five other persons. I have often hired a special messenger to travel a distance of thirty miles for eight cents. Boatmen are regularly hired to track a native boat, pulling it against the stream from Tientsin to Tungcho, a distance of one hundred and twenty-five miles, for fifty cents and their food one way. They make the return journey on foot—that is, they travel a greater distance than that separating Boston and New York for fifty cents in silver and one half of their food. Countless multitudes of Chinese earn a living by gathering offal on country roads, and it is nothing unusual to see a lively scrimmage between twelve or fifteen men and boys for the possession of a heap of horse-manure. This may serve to indicate what poverty means in China. To an immense number of the people, failure of work for one day carries with it, as an inevitable sequence, failure of any sort of food for the same period.

From the prices paid for labor, as given above, it is not a difficult matter to estimate the extremely narrow limits within which the daily expenditures of a majority of the four hundred millions of Chinese must be kept. The difficulty lies in discovering how they live at all. Their daily food consists of rice steamed, cabbage boiled in an unnecessarily large quantity of water, and for a relish, a few bits of raw turnip, pickled in a strong brine. When disposed to be very extravagant and reckless of expense, they buy a cash worth of dried watermelon seeds, and munch them as a dessert. In summer they eat raw cucumbers, skin, prickles, and all, raw carrots or turnips, or, perhaps, a melon, not wasting the rind. In certain parts of the empire wheat flour, oat, or cornmeal takes the place of rice. With this variation the description answers with entire accuracy for the food consumption of the great masses of the Chinese people—not for the beggars or the very poor, but for the common classes of industrious workingmen and their families, whether in the great cities or in the rural districts.

I once had occasion to spend the night at a Buddhist temple beautifully located in a ravine of the mountains, about a hundred miles east of Peking. It was in October, and the priests, though accustomed to entertain Chinese guests, had no other articles of food than raw chestnuts and delicious water from a spring which bubbled from the rocks within the temple enclosure. When I commented upon this meagre fare, the aged abbot in charge seemed surprised, and said : " But you don't know how fine our chestnuts are. They are not at all like ordinary fruit. Eat a pound of them and drink plenty of water, and your hunger will be satisfied." Doubtless it would.

Upon another occasion, while traveling in the western part of China with some companions, we reached, late one Saturday night, an inn where the only article of food obtainable was wheat flour moistened with water, then rolled flat and thin, cut into strips, and thrown for a moment into a kettle of boiling water. It was tasteless, tough as leather, and as indigestible. The inn furnished nothing else, nor could anything be procured in the village, though after long search an obliging native managed to provide us with some eggs. The next day our servant discovered a Chinese peddling meat upon the street, and, in spite of the day, bought some, as we were really suffering from hunger. It was already cooked, so he hastily warmed up a large portion, which was placed before us. The flavor was so suspicious, that a single mouthful satisfied our hunger and aroused our curiosity. The servant said, in answer to questions, that, while he had not inquired, he judged the meat to be beef, and that he had purchased it from an old man with a wheelbarrow load only a short distance from the inn. We went in search of the old man, whom we soon found, and with whom the following conversation took place:

"How do you do, Venerable Sir? How is trade to-day?"

"Excellent. I had a heaping wheelbarrow load, and have sold all but the few pieces that you see."

"What sort of meat are you selling? Beef?"

"No, it is not beef. I am a farmer living in a village a few miles away. I had an old mule that was taken sick and died. I could not afford to lose it, so I sold the hide and cooked the carcass, and have sold every pound of it except what you see here."

Upon another occasion, while traveling in the northwestern part of China with two companions, we lost our way. We had walked on ahead of our drivers, mules, baggage, and servants, had taken the wrong road, and in consequence found ourselves at dark on a bitter cold day in December in an inn without our own attendants, and, as we found upon counting and combining our resources, with exactly one hundred pieces of cash—about ten cents—with which to pay for food and lodging. The inn was better than the average, and was supplied with all the varieties of food which the region afforded. We had supper, lodging, and breakfast, as good in every respect as the inn or the village could have furnished at any price, paid our bill, with the usual gratuity to the servants, and had twelve cash remaining in hand. Six meals and lodging for three men were furnished for less than nine cents! But, to tell the truth, the bill of fare was wholesome, but simple in the extreme. It consisted of Irish potatoes—there called earth eggs—boiled and eaten with salt, and oatmeal gruel seasoned in the same way. The bed was the usual brick platform covered with a clean mat and made warm by a good coal fire. There was no bedding, as travelers in China always carry their own, and ours was with our mules; but arctic overshoes did duty for a pillow, and for the rest, we slept as we had traveled, and suffered no inconvenience or discomfort.

These three incidents of personal experience occurred at points distant many hundred miles each from the other, in different sections of the Chinese Empire. Two of them were met with in villages upon great highways of travel, where thousands pass and are entertained every month. They are given to enforce the statements made regarding the extremely simple habits and narrow range of food of the poorer but comparatively well-to-do classes among the Chinese. It is plain and frugal in the extreme, and even then must be bought meal by meal, as it is needed. An ordinary Chinese workingman would be far less likely to be able to purchase supplies for his family in any quantity, than a man of the same rank of life here would be to purchase several thousand dollars' worth of bonds or other securities. One of the most common sights in any city or town of China is that of a boy or girl with three or four pieces of cash in one hand and a couple of dishes of coarse pottery in the other going, with great dignity and importance, to purchase the materials for the family dinner, and the fuel with which to cook it. The bill of expenditures would run somewhat as follows: Charcoal, one cash; rice or flour, two cash; cabbage, one cash. On occasions of prosperity another cash would be spent for oil or soy, and on very rare and exceptional festive days still another would be invested in purchasing about a teaspoonful of weak alcohol, to be drank hot with the meal.

The clothing of the Chinese poor is as simple as the diet. In the summer it consists of shoes and stockings, both made of cotton cloth, and trousers, unlined, of the same material. A jacket or blouse, also of cotton, completes his apparel, but this garment is frequently omitted if the temperature will permit.

In spring and autumn the poor man wears, if he can afford them, garments of the same material lined. In the winter, in a climate like that of New York or Philadelphia, his trousers are wadded, and his upper garment is either also wadded, or is a sheepskin tanned with the wool on, which is worn next the skin. He has no knowledge of underclothing of any sort. One suit answers for all hours, since he sleeps in the same clothes in which he works. Three dollars would be more than sufficient to buy the entire summer wardrobe of what may be called a comfortably poor Chinese— that is, one at work on steady wages. Twenty-five or thirty cents would be more than the value of the rags worn by the very poor. One peculiarity

GROUP OF CHINESE WORKMEN.

of the beggar class is worthy of notice. They invariably wear shoes. The usual covering of a lusty Chinese beggar is a bowl with which to receive donations of food or money, and a pair of shoes. He may not have the bowl, but his feet are always covered. A barefooted Chinaman is never seen.

The house of the poor man in China is built either of sun-dried or broken brick laid up in mud, and roofed sometimes with tiles, but more commonly with a mixture of lime and clay spread upon reed mats. It is never more than one story in height, and for a family of five or six persons seldom consists of more than one room. It has a floor of either mud or brick, never of boards, windows of paper, and a door sufficiently open for all purposes of ventilation. It has no chimney, and no fire is used summer or winter, except the small amount necessary for the family cooking. The entire furniture consists of a table, a stool or two, a wardrobe when it can be afforded, and a raised platform of brick covered with a coarse mat of reeds, which serves for the family bed. Flues run underneath this, and the smoke and heat from the fire used in cooking passes through them, thus securing a small amount of warmth. In southern China the brick platform is replaced by one built of bamboo or some other inexpensive wood.

It is to be feared that men of Western lands, if asked the question whether, under such circumstances and conditions, life is worth living, would answer in the negative. And it could not be a matter for surprise if such abject poverty developed great selfishness, indifference to the sufferings of others, and general disregard of the common obligations of humanity; yet in simple justice it must be said that such is not the fact. In China, as elsewhere, it is not the wealthy but the poor who are most prompt and liberal, in proportion to their resources, to respond to the necessities of those even more unfortunate than themselves. Much might be written of the many pleasant phases of Chinese life among the poor, which is developed by their extreme poverty, their patience and quiet endurance, their readiness to help each other, and their faithful care, even when suffering the utmost depths of want, of the aged and infirm. It should also not be forgotten that from such homes have come, in a very large measure, the distinguished scholars and statesmen who have been the practical rulers of the nation, and have given her a literature and a history of which, in some features at least, she has no cause to be ashamed. Life has some pleasant pictures, some lessons worthy to be learned, even in the poverty and hunger of a Chinese hovel.

China has for many centuries been confronted with the exact reverse of the problem with which the United States for the greater part of its existence has had to deal. With us the practical question has been, at least until recently, by what labor-saving devices one man may be enabled to accomplish the work of ten. The result here is what might have been expected. Necessity has spurred ingenuity, and Americans lead the world in the invention of labor-saving machines of every sort.

In China the opposite question has been a subject of constant and anxious study from a period far antedating the discovery of this Western Continent. It may be stated in these words: With an excessive population, how may any given piece of

MENDER OF TUBS.

work be so divided and subdivided as to furnish the barest sustenance to the largest possible number of persons? One result of the study of this problem is also what might have been anticipated. The Chinese are the most economical race upon the face of the earth. If they lack in the broader field of ingenuity, they are easily the ingenious masters of the science and art of economics.

Absolutely nothing is wasted. The smallest rags and shreds of cloth are saved, carefully pasted together, and form the insole of shoes. Bits of woods are ingeniously glued and dovetailed into other bits, until a board or post is literally built up. Half the houses in the city of Peking are built of fragments of brick which have been in use for centuries, and may continue to do duty for centuries to come. A large business is done in the capital in making lamps from the discarded sardine, oyster, and other cans. In the country the weeds and grass by the roadside are carefully gathered by women and children, the entire surface being scratched over and over again, and this refuse does duty as fuel. The roots of corn and other grains are carefully spaded up, the earth beaten from then, and when dried in the sun they serve the same useful purpose.

In many of these lines it is cheaper to us to waste than to save, and what is true economy among the Chinese would be false economy with us. But there labor counts for little—is indeed the cheapest article in the market; hence its employment, even where the results are of the most trifling nature, is wise.

And among the poorer classes every one works. The solitary exception is the infant too young to walk, and he, safely deposited upon his back on a mat, lies quietly doubling his fists and blinking at the sun, which is his part in the labors of the day.

Certain processes in the preparation of tea and silk are reserved exclusively for women and girls, who earn from one to three cents a day by this labor. The straw braid from which our hats are made comes from one of the northern provinces of China. It is woven by women and children, who rarely can earn more than two cents a day in the work.

While the government of China makes no regular provision for the support of the pauper element among its people, it tacitly recognizes begging as a legitimate occupation. It never interferes with or restrains it. Thus, if a crowd of fifty or a hundred creatures, so filthy and diseased as to be hardly recognizable as human beings, should beset the entrance to a store or office, and refuse to move on until their demands for money were granted, it would be idle for the proprietor to appeal to the police. He would be met with the answer, "Give them what they ask. The amount is small, and then they will go away." There is a shade of reason in such a reply. Begging, like everything else, is reduced to a system in China. Beggars never go in crowds or even in pairs. Each has his district, and only calls in others when he has been repulsed, or, as he conceives, been treated with scant courtesy. He never expects more than a single cash. It is a mistake to give him this small sum too promptly, for in such case he will come again too soon. He must be kept waiting for it a certain length of time, so as to earn it ; but it is a far more serious mistake to insult him or send him away empty-handed. He will come again the day following with two or three companions, each more filthy than the other, and less than half a dollar will fail to satisfy them. If they are again refused, the place is soon fairly besieged with a throng of a hundred or more, and at least a hundred dollars must then be expended instead of the single cash which would have satisfied the solitary mendicant who first appealed for alms.

Many merchants and shopkeepers in the larger cities pay a regular monthly allowance, agreed upon. A sign, cabalistic but well understood by the begging fraternity, is written upon the doorposts of such as make this arrangement, and they are only visited by the "collector" upon a fixed day, who then receives and receipts for the commutation or blackmail; and those who decline to enter into such an arrangement very rarely refuse to give the single cash demanded, as they know by experience the results which are certain to follow.

Peking, like all Oriental cities, swarms with beggars. They are met with everywhere, in every condition of filth, and of real or counterfeit deformity or disease. They are of both sexes and all ages. Begging is with them a business, a profession, to which they are trained from infancy, and in which some attain great success. It is as easy to distinguish a professional beggar from an amateur—that is, from a man driven by misfortune to ask relief—as it is to discriminate between a horse and a mule.

Peking beggars have a regular guild or organization, presided over by a king and a queen. These officers are elective, and hence, so far as I have

CHINESE PASSENGER CART.

been able to learn, the mendicants of the capital are the only Chinese in the empire who are permitted to exercise the privileges of the ballot. The king is said never to be seen by profane eyes, but I have had a conversation with the queen, who appeared to be a respectable, well-dressed Chinese lady of sixty-five or seventy years of age. The entire city is carefully divided into districts, and no beggar is allowed to intrude upon the territory of another. Still this calling, like all others, has its black sheep. There are tramp beggars, not members of the guild, who roam everywhere in city and country, bound by no limits, and heedless of the rights of others. They are regarded with contempt as being guilty of unprofessional and discreditable conduct by those members of the fraternity who confine themselves each to his own vineyard and harvest field.

Chinese mendicants are past masters in the art of simulating disease or deformity of every sort. I was for a long time annoyed in my daily walks in Peking by a young Chinese woman, who would follow me, carrying one child and leading another. While screaming out uncouth sounds at the top of her voice, she indicated by gestures that she was deaf and dumb, the two children keeping up a sort of minor refrain by the wailing cry, " Have pity and give a cash ! Have pity and give a cash !" For some reason hard to define, I suspected that the creature had the full natural use of both her ears and mouth. In order to test the question, one day, when she was more than usually annoying and was crying after me in the midst of a crowd, I turned suddenly upon her and said something which, while not improper, would, if she could hear it, certainly make her angry. She replied instantly in remarkably good Chinese with a torrent of vile language, and then, amid roars of laughter from the crowd, she suddenly realized that she had betrayed herself, and slunk out of sight. Thereafter she always recognized me pleasantly when we met, but never begged of me.

I well remember one case among all the wretchedness and revolting sights found in the beggar class of Peking which moved my pity, and which, as a solitary exception to my rule, was for several months regularly relieved. It was an old man, ragged and shivering with cold, who sat every day by the side of the street. He was clothed in only a few rags, and thrust out in front of him were his feet, which were literally rotting off. They presented a sight too offensive for more detailed description. One day I missed the old man from his accustomed place, but walking rapidly homeward, I overtook him trudging along, and no signs of frozen feet and decomposition were visible.

"Why," said I, walking along by his side, "how can you manage to walk with those wretched feet?"

"Oh," said the old man, "they are in my bosom. It would spoil them to wear them home."

Then, without hesitation or sign of shame, he thrust his hands into his bosom and drew out a pair of socks padded with cotton in order to represent his feet as swollen and out of shape. They were made of canvas, and so accurately painted into the resemblance of feet with toenails dropping off and the flesh a mass of putrefaction, that they had deceived me in broad sunlight and on many occasions.

Naturally I was furious, and said : " I should think that an old man like you would be ashamed to swindle people in this way. Have you no trade, or are you too lazy to earn your rice in any honest fashion ?"

To which the venerable humbug replied as simply and frankly as though his recent deception had been quite respectable and praiseworthy : " Oh, yes, I am a shoemaker ; and I have been thinking about giving up this line of business, for my feet are getting to be too well known, and it does not pay as well as it did. After all, it is hard work sitting there upon the ground all day and shouting out, ' Have pity ! ' I believe that I will go back to my old trade of mending shoes."

In a day or two he appeared with his kit of tools and his bench, and asked permission to establish himself quite near the entrance of the Legation, by the side of the street, which was granted. There he cobbled shoes for nearly ten years, when he died ; and his son, who " succeeded to the title and estates," asked assistance to bury the old man, basing his plea upon the close intimacy which had so long existed between us.

CHAPTER XV.

CHINESE FINANCIAL SYSTEM.

An ounce of refined silver bullion constitutes the unit of money in the Chinese Empire. Copper cash and paper notes comprise the subsidiary currency in use among the people. Mexican dollars are used to a considerable extent in those parts of the country where foreign trade has been developed, but they are invariably valued by weight, and a large proportion of those imported soon find their way to the melting-pot, where they are refined, and whence they reappear as bullion. A variety of causes have produced this apparently absurd treatment of coins recognized as standard in weight and fineness throughout all parts of the world except China.

The Oriental merchant and man of business has a wonderfully accurate eye in determining the quality of native bullion. The signs by which he judges each piece are necessarily lacking in minted coins, and he has no proof, save what is to him a vague and unreliable assurance, that such coins contain only an invariable amount of alloy. Hence, he prefers to reduce them to the simpler primary form to which he is accustomed, and in which his keen eyes can determine at a swift glance their actual value. His own government has never received, paid, or recognized any other form of money than pure silver bullion.

A custom sprang up in the ports of southern China, where Spanish and Mexican dollars were first introduced, which, while intended to assure the natives of the reliability of these coins, had the inevitable effect to drive every one of them, sooner or later, to the refiners. Native bankers adopted the practice of stamping their firm name, with a steel die, upon the face of every dollar which passed over their counters, thus making themselves responsible for its redemption at full value. Thus one firm after another would cut its name into the face of a coin, and, under this process of authentication, the money speedily become battered out of all shape or possibility of recognition, and was literally punched full of holes. Then they ceased to pass as dollars *by count*, but were still current *by weight* for a time, their final destiny always being the melting-pot.

Some years ago a distinguished American lady, while visiting Canton, desired to draw five hundred Mexican dollars upon her letter of credit, with which to make some purchases. Her banker advised her not to take the actual coin, but to give each merchant with whom she dealt an order upon him for the amount of her purchase. He would then deduct the sum total of her expenditures from her letter of credit. As she declined to follow this course, preferring to pay her own bills, the banker brought her the required sum in a canvas bag, and spread the money out that she might by count assure herself of its correctness. It resembled nothing so much as battered bits and scraps of old tin. There was not one piece in the lot which could be counted as a dollar, or whose value could be determined except by weight; yet it was the nearest approach to "clean Mexican dollars" then obtainable at Canton.

The imperial government has its own standard of weight, called the "treasury ounce," by which it receives and disburses all sums, and it only accepts or pays bullion of ninety-eight per cent fineness; but it exercises no scrutiny over the commercial transactions of its subjects. There are no laws calculated to regulate the weight of an ounce or the quality of bullion; hence there is an utter lack of uniformity in both of these essential particulars. Making no allowance for individual attempts to get or give more or less than fair weight, there are five different ounces recognized and in daily use in Peking alone. These are the "two-ounce" weight, as it is called, in which ninety-eight ounces are reckoned as one hundred; in other words, it is two per cent short of true measure. This is the lightest of all. Next comes the "commercial ounce;" then what is known as the "official ounce;" then the "treasury ounce," already mentioned; and last, and heaviest of all, the "customs ounce." This last is a modern innovation, having been in use for less than thirty years. It is the measure by which import and export duties are levied and paid. For some inexplicable reason it is heavier than the ounce adopted by the government.

The ounces in use in the capital differ, again, from those used in other cities and districts of the empire, which in turn differ among themselves. There is no standard ounce weight in use everywhere for weighing silver, excepting the treasury weight, and that is only used in transactions with the government. That such a lack of uniformity should produce great inconvenience and no little uncertainty in the results of business operations is evident. Bankers and those who have occasion to remit sums of money, either by drafts or in bulk, from one point to another, are familiar with the difference in the ounce weights between the two cities, and make the necessary allowances.

Custom, in one of the peculiar freaks which it so often exhibits in China, has established a rule that certain classes of transactions shall be paid in a certain kind of ounce weight, if no particular weight is named in the agreement. Thus, in Peking, house rent may be paid in the lightest ounce; bills due to merchants or shopkeepers are payable in the market, or "commercial" ounce, while other accounts must be balanced with a heavier measure. It is impossible to discover the origin or reason of this rule of trade, nor does it prevent a native entitled, according to its dictum, to the lightest ounce, from claiming the heaviest. It exercises a sort of moral restraint upon him, with the result that, after a due expenditure of argument and expostulation, he will magnanimously, and with great show of virtue, abate his original demand and accept what this custom prescribes, and all that he has at any moment, in the height of his vocal gymnastics, expected to receive. No person exceeds the Chinaman in his belief in the old saying that it never does any harm to try.

Government has nothing whatever to do with refining silver bullion. This process is entirely in the hands of private individuals or firms. It is commonly cast into an oval form resembling in some faint degree the shape of a Chinese shoe, and hence known among foreign residents as a "shoe" of silver. The more common size averages about fifty ounces in weight, though smaller ingots of about ten ounces are also cast. These regular sizes are chopped or cut into smaller bits or fragments in order to make the exact sum needed in any payment. Refiners stamp their firm name upon the surface of each block of bullion and a mark indicating the purity of the metal, and in the case of well-known firms this mark may be safely accepted as correct. As has already been said, Chinese merchants and men of business have a marvelously keen eye and accurate judgment of the fineness of any piece of bullion cast according to their methods. The mould is made principally of asbestos. The metal is poured into this, given a single sudden shake, and then dumped. Upon the surface of the "shoe" will be found a number of tiny waves, and upon the sides and bottom a number of pin-holes in the metal. These furnish the two most important tests of the purity of the metal. The greater the number and the less the size of these waves and pin-holes, the higher the grade of the silver.

An essential part of every business transaction

of any amount in China is the stipulation fixing the weight of the ounce to be employed and the quality of the bullion in which the specified sum is to be paid or received. It was once my duty to receive from the magistrate of a Chinese city several hundred ounces of silver as indemnity for injuries received by certain American citizens at the hands of a mob. A written agreement had been duly executed in which it was specified that the amount fixed upon should be paid in treasury ounces of commercially pure bullion. At the time set for payment, the sum was brought carefully wrapped and sealed in parcels, each endorsed as containing fifty ounces.

Knowing that some Chinese officials were fond of driving sharp bargains, I had provided myself with weights known to be accurate, and taking a parcel at random, I opened and weighed it. It was of poor silver—not more than third grade—and weighed exactly forty-seven ounces. An examination of a second and a third parcel gave exactly similar results. The entire amount was returned to the underlings who had brought it, to be taken back to their master, with the message that, if within one hour he failed to fulfill his promise to pay the sum agreed upon in pure silver of treasury weight, our arrangement for the settlement of the case would be canceled, and his conduct reported to his superiors at Peking. My message was promptly delivered, and brought an immediate response in the shape of silver which, in weight and fineness, more than fulfilled the terms of the agreement.

On the afternoon of the same day, when I went by invitation to dine with this magistrate, he met me at the door with an open, hearty laugh, and the remark, "I tried to cheat you with poor silver and light weight this morning, because I thought that you, being a foreigner, would not know the difference, but I found that you knew even better than I." Then he told me, as a huge joke, that he had provided and weighed out the requisite amount in each weight and quality of silver, and sent the low quality and deficient weight first, hoping that the trick would pass unnoticed, but ready to make his promise good if it became necessary to do so.

Chinese cash are cast in moulds, and not minted. Their use as money dates back almost to the beginning of time. The first cash is recorded and described as having been made about 2300 B.C., which would be about the time of the Flood. The three specimens reproduced in the accompanying cut were current more than two thousand years ago. The largest, called a "sword cash" among the Chinese, from its peculiar shape, was in use as money at the time when the Great Wall of China was built, or about 221 B.C. The circular specimen was coined and used about the time that King David reigned in Jerusalem. It represents in general form and outline the cash used at the present time, the only difference being in the raised figures or characters, which give the name of the emperor under whose reign it was coined, and a Chinese phrase which may be translated "current coin of the realm." The cultivated Chinese are enthusi-

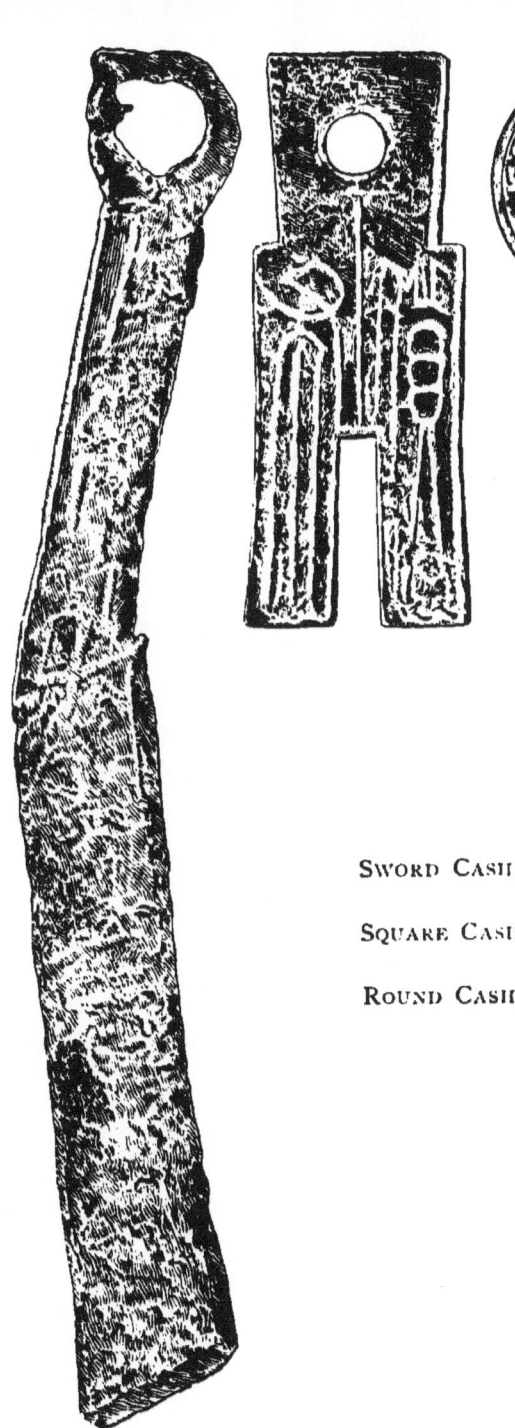

Sword Cash, B.C. 221.

Square Cash, A.D. 1.

Round Cash, B.C. 1085.

astic collectors of old coins, and genuine specimens command high prices. Pieces which date back not more than three or four hundred years are not considered as antique, and will frequently be found upon strings of cash in current use. It is no uncommon thing to find cash cast half a century before the discovery of America still passing from hand to hand in the petty transactions of daily life.

The theoretical cash is a disk of pure copper, about three quarters of an inch in diameter, having a square hole in the centre for convenience in stringing. It weighs fifty-eight grains Troy, and is equivalent in value to one thousandth part of a standard ounce of refined silver bullion. Mints for casting cash are established at Peking and in each provincial capital under the supervision of the treasury. Great care is taken to prevent counterfeiting and private minting, and the men employed in the works are never allowed to leave the premises, night or day, except at rare intervals and under special precautions. The chief security against counterfeiting, however, exists in the fact that no coin resembling the genuine cash can be produced at less cost, and hence there is little or no profit in any imitation.

The government of China has, however, not been wiser than its Western neighbors in attempts, in past centuries, to manipulate its currency, to give fictitious values to its coins, and, in general, to create a valuable something out of nothing. Centuries ago it tried the " fiat money" scheme, and issued unlimited quantities of paper money. Three hundred years before the first bank-note was issued in Europe—that is to say, in A.D. 1368—the people of China were called upon to use paper money made theoretically valuable by the will of the emperor. In an absolute autocracy such a scheme ought to succeed, if anywhere ; yet it went the way of all such schemes, and now a solitary specimen of the issue is to be found in the British Museum, having gained a value through age which it would never have obtained in any other way. The numerous brilliant discoveries in modern finance, which are being exploited in so many quarters, are veritable ancient history among the Chinese. Every one of them has been tried, and every one has failed. And the Chinese Government has long since proved by repeated experiment that, among its people at least, no promise will pass current without a solid backing of fact, and that no human power, whether it be imperial or common, can force any article upon the people at a higher valuation than its current market price.

The foreign traveler or student in China often stumbles upon the relics of these financial experiments, sometimes to his amusement, and more often to the utter confusion of his cash account. The experiments most in evidence at the present day have been made with the cash. As has been stated, in theory each piece should be equivalent in value to one thousandth of an ounce of silver. Reduction in the amount of copper contained in each piece has invariably and immediately affected their current value. To-day the average value of the cash is eighteen hundred pieces to an ounce of silver, though the rate fluctuates from day to day, and each large city or commercial centre throughout the empire has its Chamber of Commerce or Board of Trade, which meets daily and determines the exchangeable value of cash for silver for each day's business.

One brilliant imperial financier, by a single stroke of his vermilion pencil, doubled the amount of money current in his empire. He decreed that each piece of cash should be counted as two. The will of the august son of Heaven was obeyed throughout the greater portion of China, though in some sections the people declined to be parties to any such nonsense; but wherever the doubling process was accepted, it was carried a point beyond the anticipations of the imperial mind. It required exactly twice as many nominal pieces of cash to purchase an ounce of silver as before. In traveling through the empire at the present time, one ignorant of this bit of history may be perplexed by finding that at one village he will be offered, say, thirty-six hundred cash for an ounce of silver, while at the next, perhaps distant less than a dozen miles, he will be able to obtain only eighteen hundred pieces for the same amount of bullion. If he sells in each place and then counts his cash, he will find that he received exactly the same number of actual pieces in each. In the one village the imperial process of doubling had been accepted, but the price of every article of merchandise had also been doubled, leaving the result of all monetary transactions absolutely unchanged. In the second village the sober-minded, practical celestials had quietly declined to lend their sanction to an imperial absurdity.

Another emperor, in a time of financial stringency, determined to coin cash of iron instead of copper. These the people unanimously and sturdily refused to accept at any rate of exchange, and the soldiers to whom they were paid simply threw them away. There are points outside the walls of Peking where a peck of these souvenirs of imperial folly may easily be gathered. They lie there in the sand, valueless even as curiosities.

This attempt to substitute iron cash for copper has left a curious impression upon the monetary system of certain parts of the empire—an impression which is worthy of notice, since it illustrates the fact that in China the will of the people is the final law, more commanding and decisive than the dictum of any emperor, and the other fact that the Oriental disposition is accommodating as well as determined. In the districts referred to, a variable number of cash is reckoned as a hundred. In one market town I found that seventy-seven pieces were counted as a hundred; in another, eighty-five; in a third, seventy-two, and in a fourth, only sixty-one. The explanation of this strange and perplexing medley was very simple. When the iron cash were issued, the people had refused to accept them. Then followed a discussion and an ultimate compromise between the people and the local authorities. The authorities had proposed that out of every hundred pieces, fifty of iron and fifty of copper be included. This had been refused. A dicker had followed, with the final result that, while in not a single town were any iron cash forced into circulation, the people had consented to count seventy-seven pieces of copper cash as one hundred in one town, eighty-five as one hundred in another, and so on, the compliant spirit of the people being exactly measured by the gap between the nominal and actual hundred pieces of money; but here there was absolutely no other result effected than an added perplexity in keeping accounts. If in selling silver bullion I was forced to receive only seventy-seven cash for a nominal hundred, I received in exact proportion more of those nominal hundreds for each ounce of the precious metal. On the other hand, in purchasing any article, the price was gauged to correspond to this difference between name and fact. The Chinaman who bought rice got only seventy-seven cash worth for his nominal hundred cash.

The most recent attempt to tamper with Chinese currency was an order directing the coinage of a large piece, which should pass as equivalent to twenty pieces of ordinary size. It was so stamped. The Chinese found it to be equal to a trifle less than four of the coins formerly in use. It has never become current anywhere in the empire except at the capital, and there it passes for its actual, not its stamped value.

The small value of the cash, and the inconvenience of making payments in them or in silver, have forced paper money into use in all Chinese cities and towns of any considerable size. These notes are issued by private bankers or "cash shops," as they are called, have a purely local circulation, and are neither guaranteed nor recognized by the government. They are redeemable on demand in cash or bullion at the holder's option. The authorities require security from all persons who propose to issue such notes, and in case of failure of a local bank of issue, proceedings are taken against the proprietors for debt exactly as would be with any other class of insolvents. Failures among these bankers are of comparatively rare occurrence. The necessity of these notes may be seen in the fact that bullion comes in blocks weighing nearly four pounds each, and worth about seventy Mexican dollars. Cash are even more inconvenient, since a dollar's worth of Peking cash would comprise nearly seven hundred pieces, each the size of an American half dollar.

The illustration reproduces two Peking banknotes, the larger worth about two dollars, and the smaller about forty cents. They are partly written and partly printed from wooden blocks on thin, coarse, but strong paper. As a safeguard against counterfeiting, each note is laid upon the blank page of a book kept for the purpose, and stamps and written lines are placed at haphazard partly upon the page and partly upon the bill. The page is then numbered and dated to correspond to the note. Crude as this method may appear, it has been found so efficient that counterfeit notes are almost unknown.

A curious vagary of Chinese financiering made its appearance in Peking in 1883. A small panic had been caused by the failure of two large banks. One of the results of the general alarm was the unwillingness of other bankers, whose standing was above suspicion, to give as much for an ounce of silver in their own notes as they would in cash.

PEKING BANK-NOTES.

They would pay as high as fifteen per cent more in money than in their promises to pay—promises which they might not be called upon to redeem in a year. No plausible explanation of this peculiar state of affairs was ever given. The Secretary of the Treasury confessed his inability to understand it. It continued for fully two years, and was considered sufficiently serious to warrant the issue of an order by the authorities directing bankers to make no discrimination, in their offers for silver, between giving their notes or cash in payment. This order, like most others touching financial questions, had no valuable effect. But it is only in China that a man, in making payment for an article purchased, is willing to give fifteen per cent more in cash than in a promissory note.

Banks of exchange are common throughout China, and remittances may be made by them to all parts of the country.

Under the theory of the imperial government, elsewhere given, all real and personal property within the limits of the empire belongs to the Emperor as the father of his people, the head of the Chinese family. What he needs he may take, when, how, and of whom he will. Under this theory the government has, and can contract, no domestic debt, since a man cannot borrow what is his own. In times of special necessity special levies of so-called voluntary contributions are made, and honorary titles and degrees are conferred upon those loyal Sons of Han who contribute cheerfully and largely to the needs of the throne.

The nominal rate of taxation upon any particular object is small, and not subject to sudden changes. The land tax averages about twenty-five cents per acre, and produces an annual revenue of more than

$150,000,000. This is the largest amount received from any one source. Salt is a government monopoly, and yields a large revenue. There is a variety of other forms of taxation, and without going into details it may be said that the imposts are so arranged that, while under the terms of the law they would bear heavily upon none, they reach every person in the empire, and compel each to bear his share in the support of the government.

It is, however, quite impossible to determine what the total revenues may be. No person either within or without the empire can fix the sum with even approximate accuracy. That it is large is evident; how large is a question that cannot be answered. The methods of collection, the division of receipts between the central government and local authorities, the percentages legally or illegally retained by collectors, and a dozen other factors of uncertainty, vex the problem and render it impossible of solution.

Certain of the taxes are payable in kind. The rice-producing provinces, for example, send immense quantities of this grain each year to Peking, where it is stored in the imperial granaries, and issued as a ration to the Manchu militiamen who are quartered in and near the capital. The Grand Canal, a national work, only less noteworthy and of far more practical value than the famous Great Wall, was built to furnish an inland waterway for this rice. It was commenced in the seventh century and completed in the fourteenth. It extends from Peking to Hang Chow, a distance of nearly seven hundred miles, though natural streams are utilized for a part of this distance. While it is not kept in proper repair, it is still in use, and large fleets of grain-bearing junks traverse it each year. It is also used to a very large extent for local and private traffic.

Silk-producing provinces, in like manner, pay a portion of their taxes in raw and manufactured silk. The tea districts pay in tea, and the outlying provinces of Mongolia furnish horses for the cavalry and for other lines of imperial service.

A large portion of the revenue is remitted to the capital by bills of exchange, but from certain of the provinces the bullion is brought in bulk, and in a manner at once primitive and peculiar. Long lines of open carts may be seen coming into the city covered with the dust and grime of travel. Each has a small triangular flag of imperial yellow color flying over it, and a soldier as guard. Each cart appears to be loaded with the old-fashioned wooden pump logs, each of which is banded spirally from end to end with iron, and covered with many strips of paper bearing Chinese seals and endorsements. Each log is composed of two longitudinal sections, and is hollow to within a few inches of either end. This space is snugly packed with fifty-ounce blocks of silver bullion, which has been brought in this manner many hundreds of miles to its destination in the imperial treasury.

The grave point of weakness and danger in the Chinese financial system, or lack of system, lies, so far as the government revenues are concerned, in the free opportunities which are afforded for extortion, illegal exactions from the people, and every form of official robbery. It is safe to say that no tax is collected and paid over to the treasury in the exact amount stipulated by law. The subject invariably pays more than he ought, and the Emperor as invariably receives less than his due. And if the exact total of all sums collected for public purposes from every source in any year could be compared with the corresponding total actually devoted to public purposes in the same period of time, the enormous divergence between the two sums would astonish the world.

The central government is aware, to some extent at least, of the pressing need of a reform in this direction, and has often expressed a desire to adopt, for example, some exact system of coinage which should protect both itself and its subjects from the abuses so safely perpetrated at present. The local officials are, almost to a man, opposed to a change which would cut off a large part of their revenue by rendering illegal levies dangerous, if not impossible. In 1877 the diplomatic representatives at Peking presented a joint memorandum upon this subject to the Chinese Cabinet. The paper was drawn with great care and distinguished ability. The Cabinet in response frankly admitted the force of the arguments employed, and expressed its anxiety to carry out the reforms suggested. It, however, added that, in accordance with the invariable rule of the imperial government in dealing with questions affecting all parts of the nation, the document must be referred to the various provincial authorities for consideration and their report, which would be communicated to the several legations. In due time these reports were so furnished, and they were, without exception, hostile to any change.

The warmest friends of China, those who believe with surest confidence in her future, wait with anxiety for a change in these matters, realizing, as they do, that such a change is an essential preliminary to any important development of the national life or power.

"NO THOROUGHFARE."

www.ingramcontent.com/pod-product-compliance
Lightning Source LLC
Chambersburg PA
CBHW020221240426
43672CB00006B/377